MW00667545

The Winona Ryder Scrapbook

The Winona

Ryder Scrapbook

EDITED BY

SCOTT AND BARBARA SIEGEL

A Citadel Press Book

PUBLISHED BY CAROL PUBLISHING GROUP

Copyright © 1997 by Siegel & Siegel Ltd.

All rights reserved. No part of this book may be reproduced in any form, except by a newspaper or magazine reviewer who wishes to quote brief passages in connection with a review.

A Citadel Press Book
Published by Carol Publishing Group
Citadel Press is a registered trademark of Carol Communications, Inc.

Editorial, sales and distribution, and rights and permissions inquiries should be addressed to Carol Publishing Group, 120 Enterprise Avenue, Secaucus, N.J. 07094.

In Canada: Canadian Manda Group, One Atlantic Avenue, Suite 105, Toronto, Ontario M6K 3E7

Carol Publishing Group books may be purchased in bulk at special discounts for sales promotion, fund-raising, or educational purposes. Special editions can be created to specifications. For details, contact Special Sales Department, Carol Publishing Group, 120 Enterprise Avenue, Secaucus, N.J. 07094.

Design by Cindy LaBreacht

Photos appearing on contents page are credited where they appear in the book.
Manufactured in the United States of America
10 9 8 7 6 5 4 3 2 1

Library of Congress Cataloging-in-Publication Data
The Winona Ryder scrapbook / edited by Scott & Barbara Siegel.
        p.   cm.
    Includes bibliographical references.
    ISBN 0-8065-1883-9
    1. Ryder, Winona, 1971-   . 2. Motion picture actors and
actresses—United States—Biography.   I. Siegel, Scott. II. Siegel, Barbara.
PN2287.R94W56   1997
791.43'028'092—dc21
[B]   97- 8681
                                                                                    CIP

Frontispiece: The look that could launch a thousand movies. PHOTO COURTESY OF MOVIE STAR NEWS. Title page: PHOTO COURTESY OF MOVIE STAR NEWS.

Cliff and Ellen Forever

Contents

A teen publicity shot that is oh so feminine. PHOTO COURTESY OF MOVIE STAR NEWS.

Winona's genius is that she retains her innocence even as a woman.
PHOTO COURTESY OF MOVIE STAR NEWS.

This is the look that
launched her in Tim
Burton's *Beetlejuice.*
PHOTO COURTESY OF PHOTOFEST.

In *The Age of Innocence,*
Winona plays May Welland,
a supporting role in the
critically acclaimed Martin
Scorsese movie that put her
firmly on the Hollywood A-
list. PHOTO COURTESY OF PHOTOFEST.

Winona played the serious daughter in *Mermaids,* the responsible young lady who was at odds with her ditzy mother (Cher).

PHOTO BY KERRY HAYES, ORION PICTURES, © 1990.

Great Balls of Fire was obviously a real eye-opener for Winona.

PHOTO COURTESY OF PHOTOFEST.

On the set of *Boys,* Winona and Lukas Haas are given instructions by director Stacy Cochran.

PHOTO BY DEMMIE TODD, © BUENA VISTA PICTURES DISTRIBUTION, INC.

Why Winona?

> "On screen Winona stands out like a polar bear on black velvet."
>
> —TIMOTHY LEARY
> ABOUT HIS
> GODDAUGHTER

Opposite: This is Winona in full flower at the 1996 Academy Awards. She's brought style and glamour back to Hollywood.
PHOTO BY LISA ROSE, GLOBE PHOTOS, INC., © 1996.

Above: PHOTO COURTESY OF MOVIE STAR NEWS.

She's been compared to a modern-day Natalie Wood—someone who has blossomed from a frail but strong-willed child star into a legendary actress. She's also been compared to Elizabeth Taylor (but without the addictions), to Drew Barrymore (but with more class), and to Audrey Hepburn (but with a greater variety of roles.)

Winona Ryder is only in her mid-twenties, yet she has perfected a range of roles that any actress in her twilight years would be proud of. And it only gets better. It's been said she dethroned Molly Ringwald as today's teen heart-throb; that she is the heiress to Madonna's counterculture icon status; that she is the nineties answer to Margaret O'Brien; yet none of those comparisons seem to do justice to the talent that is so well packed in this diminutive five-foot, four-inch powerhouse weighing barely 100 pounds.

Winsome Winona is the definition of teen angst in many of her roles without ever playing a cheerleader or a prom queen. She's the dark, death-welcoming teen in Tim Burton's *Beetlejuice* and the reluctant murderous wannabe best friend in Michael Lehmann's *Heathers*. She's the child bride in *Great Balls of Fire!*, a cab driver in *Night on Earth,* an android alien fighter in *Alien 4,* and a torture victim in *The House of the Spirits.*

No two Winona roles are alike, yet somehow they are all the same. Many of her characters write in a diary or journal, just as she does in real life, and she usually plays the geek or the odd person out, again, much as she is in real life.

Winona is a feisty, strong independent young woman, but plays the object of men's desires in *Boys, Bram Stoker's Dracula, The Age of Innocence,* and *Reality Bites.* She recreates herself each time; she reinvents herself within films that are as engagingly offbeat as she is.

But, most important, she is the soul of all her films; usually capturing the part of the spokesperson, the narrator, the person through whom the story is told. She is also like that in life. Though she may first appear to be the distant observer, more often she is the instigator, the motivator, the raison d'être for the whole story.

She's the soul of all of the Little Women as Jo, and the mother to her mother (played by Cher) in *Mermaids.* She's fiercely insightful in her small role in *Night on Earth,* as well as in *Looking for Richard* (which took the January 1996 Sundance Festival by storm), in *Boys,* and most certainly in *The Crucible.* She's strong, she's sexy, and she's her own person—as much in her filmwork as in her real life.

She is aware how much men want her both on screen and off, and it makes her uncomfortable. She lost her virginity twice on screen, in *Great Balls of Fire!* and in *Mermaids.*

She marries the great vampire Dracula, almost marries the great ghost Beetlejuice, and does marry Daniel Day-Lewis in *Age of Innocence* and Jerry Lee Lewis (Dennis Quaid) in *Great Balls of Fire!* She falls in love with a retarded man in *Square Dance,* is shunned by a prepubescent boy in *Lucas,* and is ignored in *Welcome Home, Roxy Carmichael.* Yet she transforms the scissor-handed monster in *Edward Scissorhands* into a hopeless romantic and converts rebel Kiefer Sutherland into a full-blooded activist in *1969.*

She's had some of the most handsome men in Hollywood, at least in her movies. Her lover in *Reality Bites* is Ethan Hawke, Daniel Day-Lewis (for the second time) in *The Crucible,* and Antonio Banderas in *The House of the Spirits.* Engaged to intensely hot new star Dermot Mulroney in *How to Make an American Quilt,* she is seduced in the same film by burgeoning new star Johnathon Schaech, who later made a hit in the Tom Hanks directorial debut of *That Thing You Do!*

Winona has chosen to perform in trendy black comedies at an age when she should be doing silly teenage high school films. But because she has avoided the glibness of that genre, she is now described in the press as "the leading anti-heroine of her generation."

That's why she continues to be one of the most popular stars on the information superhighway. There are more than 100 web sites with her name on them, from Indonesia to the Netherlands, from Japan to Hungary. (She did have a personal internet e-mail address on America Online, but she received so much mail that she went incognito.)

She's been honored for her work, but critics all agree it's only the beginning. She has been nominated twice for an Oscar, the first time as Best Supporting Actress in *The Age of Innocence* and the second time as Best Actress in *Little Women*. Among some of her other most notable awards are a Golden Globe nomination for Best Supporting Actress in both *Mermaids* and *The Age of Innocence* (she won for *The Age of Innocence*). Her roles are so eclectic, so above her age, so mature, that *Entertainment Weekly* once declared her the Actress Most in Need of Playing a Lowlife.

And that's just her films. She's immortalized in rock songs; she's made miscellaneous appearances on television, including an insightful documentary of one of her favorite painters, *Georgia O'Keeffe: Portrait of an Artist*. She joined the famous cadre of stars, including Michael Jackson and Elizabeth Taylor, by guest-starring on an episode of *The Simpsons* which first aired on September 11, 1994. Episode number 105, called "Lisa's Rival," has Winona playing a classmate, Alison, who constantly competes with the brainy daughter of Homer Simpson.

Her appearances in music videos are legendary. Naturally, she's portrayed as a sniper in the Soul Asylum video for their song "Without A Trace" and she's in *Mermaid* costar Cher's video "It's In His Kiss (The Shoop-Shoop Song)." But her crowning glory is Mojo Nixon's odd song "Debbie Gibson Is Pregnant With My Two-Headed Love Child," where she ends up sharing a motel bed with a Spuds MacKenzie lookalike. She also had a cameo appearance in a concert special, "Philips DCC Presents Zoo-TV Featuring U2." She was even nominated for a Grammy for her reading of *The Diary of a Young Girl*, the autobiography of Anne Frank.

At home you can find her listening to KROQ-FM in Los Angeles or popping in the tape of Milkman's *Punk Rock Girl*, or driving off to explore spooky old abandoned houses around the city.

Her influences vary widely. She says she used to idolize former Los Angeles Dodgers second baseman Steve Sax to the point of writing "Winona Sax" on her schoolbooks, but because loyalty is of undying importance to her, she detested him after he went off to the Yankees. Where she says she once worshipped him now she says, "I burst into

Practicing her come-hither look. PHOTO COURTESY OF MOVIE STAR NEWS.

tears. The fucking Yankees. I would never do that if I was a Dodger. It's morally reprehensible."

Loyalty and friendship she holds most valuable. That's why she works with the same people again and again (director Tim Burton, actor Daniel Day-Lewis, producer Denise DiNovi), and she gets her friends (Samantha Mathis, Claire Danes, singer/boyfriend David Pirner, even Johnny Depp) roles in her films. Actor Richard E. Grant says the reason that he appears in *Bram Stoker's Dracula* and *The Age of Innocence* is solely because Winona loved his portrayal as the lead in *Withnail and I,* and she's responsible for pushing the British film's recent re-release in the United States.

She's determined to talk about the people who influenced her, helping her to become what she is today, including the pop-culture crowd of Harper Lee, Ellen Gilchrist, the Replacements, Truman Capote, Kirk Gibson, Greta Garbo, Ian McEwan, and especially author J. D. Salinger. "My all-time favorite novel is *Catcher in the Rye.* It's my bible," she says. "I bet I've read it fifty times. It was my dad's favorite book, too. I was crushed when I found out a whole generation discovered it before me."

> *"I don't think she's into deep self-analysis. She doesn't think about it, she just does it."*
>
> —WINONA'S FRIEND LISA FALK

Her politically active parents, Michael and Cindy Horowitz, and her funky godfather, Timothy Leary, still hold the most influence in her life. They are the ones who planted the seeds of her activism, causing her to do things like start the Polly Klaas foundation (see chapter 13 for more details).

She's offbeat, yes (she hates being called "quirky") but she's never a rebel. She's never going to pose nude, or be in a drug rehab program, or commit suicide, or even get married before her time. Standing at the Griffith Observatory where James Dean and Natalie Wood performed a climactic scene in *Rebel Without a Cause,* Winona confesses, "I've experimented with stuff. People are curious, but curiosity is one thing and destroying yourself is something else."

She declares, at a time when her close friend actor Robert Downey, Jr. is struggling with his drug-addiction demons, "I don't do things that are harmful to me. I've already seen actors who have been very destructive. As soon as they are a success they get messed up."

The song "Qué Será, Será" frames her signature film *Heathers,* and it clearly has made a mark on Winona's life. She's not without critics, but she takes it all in stride.

Noted *Los Angeles Times* film critic Sheila Benson has trashed Winona's favorite film, *Heathers,* by saying, "No amount of production sheen or acting skills seems excuse enough for the film's scabrous morality or its unprincipled viciousness."

Such criticism comes from the same people (Winona muses) that asked her at a 1991 press junket, "Why are you always playing teenagers?" She answered curtly, "I'm nineteen. What am I supposed to do, play a judge?"

Yet most critics rave about her, labeling her performances deft and remarkable and praising her "fascinatingly offbeat comic timing." *Variety* called her "fetching." *Cosmopolitan* dubbed her "wonderful." "She's a cheesy, tacky, nervous, geeky, defensive, pampered, privileged midget freak," said *Rolling Stone,* and *Premiere* called her a "torchbearer for teen angst and a source of heat for older viewers."

She's been directed by the best: Martin Scorsese, Francis Ford Coppola, Jim Jarmusch, Tim Burton. She doesn't need to be a drama queen, she's not a schmoozer, she can appear impatient, moody, and silent. She doesn't care how she dresses, she doesn't mince her words. She's her own person and people respect her for that.

"Ninety percent [of people] get persuaded by people around them—'You have to do this part, work with this director.' But you can have fifty people in a room telling Winona what to do, and if she doesn't want to do it, forget it," says her close friend Denise DiNovi, who has produced three of her movies.

She says she wants to do *Little Women,* and she got it done. She doesn't want to do *Godfather III* so she doesn't do it and her replacement in the role, Sofia Coppola, bombs. She pushes a script in front of Francis Ford Coppola's nose and stars in *Bram Stoker's Dracula,* helping him to revive his sagging career.

One of her directors, Ben Stiller, notes, "It's funny—girls really like her, and guys really like her. Every guy I've ever talked to has a crush on her."

Costar Janeane Garofalo insists, "I've noticed that even little, little kids like her. I think Winona's the poster girl of every Trekkie, every computer nerd, every information superhighway addict, every comedyhead and every comic book collector. And athletes, too."

Her fans can write her, and many do. She'll try to answer, if she has time, but she'll definitely read the letters. She likes to read—and respond to—what her fans want.

"I just want to do things that matter," Winona says.

"And as you'll see, in less than three decades of life, she's done plenty.

The Winona Ryder Scrapbook

Not Just a Town in Minnesota

"Somebody wrote 'Winona Ryder is my role model' and I was really flattered, but then I got to thinking about it and I started getting scared. I'm really going to have to watch what I do, watch what I say. I feel an instinctive responsibility."

—WINONA TO GODFATHER
TIMOTHY LEARY IN 1989

Winona is looking quite womanly, and why not? The affair with Depp was out in the open. PHOTO COURTESY OF MOVIE STAR NEWS.

*H*er real name is Winona Laura Horowitz, born on the twenty-ninth of October in 1971. She was born fifty miles outside of Minneapolis in Winona, Minnesota, where she and her family still spend Christmas visiting relatives. It was this town that gave her parents, Cindy Palmer, a writer and video artist, and Michael Horowitz, a rare-book collector, her name. Winona is also the name of an Indian sex goddess, a fact her parents came across while writing a book about shamanism just before she was born. Her middle name, Laura, was taken from Utopian idealist Aldous Huxley's wife's name.

Most of her close friends call her Noni, her nickname since birth, and to this day you'll read quotes or hear stars who have befriended her all calling her Noni.

Winona is the third of four children; her siblings include an older half-sister, Sunyata, who is interested in being a model, an older half-brother, Jubal, who is into

3

heavy metal, and a brother, Yuri, who loves baseball.

Her mother, Cindy, lived in San Francisco in Haight-Ashbury with her first husband and took part in the first "be-in" of self-discovery, macrobiotics, Buddhism, Utopia, and the philosophies of Huxley. This was the marriage that produced Winona's sister, Sunyata, whose name comes from *The Tibetan Book of the Dead,* and brother, Jubal, whose name came to Cindy in a dream. They are three and two years older than Winona, respectively. Cindy married antique-book collector Michael Horowitz in 1970, and a year later moved for a short time to Minnesota where they had Winona. Then, two years after Winona, Yuri, who was named after the first Russian cosmonaut, was born.

Soon after Winona arrived, the family returned to San Francisco. In an oddly open way, the family shared a house in the Haight with Cindy's first ex-husband. While she lived in San Francisco, Winona attended Zen preschool or sat and watched her father drink coffee at the Cafe Trieste with his friend, Beat poet Allen Ginsberg.

Her childhood was mostly spent on a ranch with other families in Mendocino County near San Francisco, and later her family moved to Petaluma, California, where the 1973 classic film *American Graffiti* was shot.

She was always a thin, gaunt child, never growing any larger than five-foot, four-inches and never weighing more than 103 pounds with a waist that measures only seventeen inches around. She has probing deep brownish hazel eyes, and her eyes sometimes seem to change color depending on how she's lit. Her hair color remains the fodder of debate among fans. It's brown, but the star herself says her natural hair was more blond and she dyed it because she thought she "looked weird" with such "pale skin and dark eyes and light hair."

As a child she chewed so many vitamin C tablets that she once told her mother that a burglar had stolen them. (Winona was forever known for exaggeration.) The parents hid vitamin bottles on the top shelves of the cabinets which might as well have been the Alps to the young girl. One day, an earthquake hit while she was climbing up to the top shelf to get the vitamins and Winona recounted, "I thought it was God punishing me and I stopped lying [about the vitamins] for about four years."

In her early days she was surrounded by pop culture intelligentsia like Leary and Ginsberg; the latter first introduced the young girl to the work of Louisa May Alcott in an anthology of writings he put together.

Leary, the Harvard drug guru, first got to know Winona during his exile in Switzerland. Winona's father worked with Leary for two decades archiving his works and publishing a 300-page bibliography of his writings. After Leary posed for a picture while holding Winona at one week old, Leary prophetically wrote on it: "I welcome a new Buddha to planet Earth."

When Winona was seven years old, after the family moved to a communal ranch, Winona looked up at her Uncle Tim and announced, "I always wanted to get to know you better because I heard you were a mad scientist." He soon took her to her first Dodger game.

"Winona has so many talents that I hope to emulate her," said Leary, whom she chose as her godfather. "She is modest, changeable, solid, witty, wise, thoughtful, exuberant, intense, bouncy, passionate," Leary clicked off like a list of Boy Scout traits.

From the time she was eight years old, she remembered wanting to act. Her mother, who sometimes kept her home from school to watch movies, was responsible for this ambition. Her mother ran a funky movie house in Elk, California near their ranch, and Winona admitted, "Ever since I can remember I've been obsessed with movies. There were couches and beds in the theater and people would pay fifty cents or a dollar to come in. I saw *A Face in the Crowd* and *East of Eden* there."

Winona loved all kinds of movies, particularly the *film noir* of the 1940s. Winona put up black bedsheets on her bedroom windows so she could watch movies in the dark.

"I wanted to live in a theater," Winona said. "You know, take out the seats, put in a bathtub. In my early years I had a lot of time to watch films. I didn't have a single friend. I had a lot of imagination. That kept me company."

She acted out a lot of films, sometimes with her family. Her first role, at eight years old, was Catwoman in a family show of *Batman.* That's when the acting bug bit hard. Later, she played Auntie Em in a summer workshop production of *The Wizard of Oz.* She recalled, "I realized that this is what I wanted to do for the rest of my life."

Life on the ranch wasn't like hanging out with a bunch of hippies as it's been portrayed in some press reports, but more like communally existing with intelligent liberal beatniks who pooled their resources for economic reasons. Some people referred to her early life as living on a commune, but she hated categorizing it that way. "It was just a way to tag it, so people labeled it as a commune because people wanted to define it as that," Winona complained. "They [some of the press] wanted to make me out as a flower child; it wasn't really all drugs and nudity like that."

The buildings on the ranch's three hundred acres all had names, and the seven other families who lived nearby worked cooperatively on the land. Winona's family lived in a house dubbed the Mansion; other buildings on the property were the A-Frame and the Cabin. Even the fields had special names.

"There was no heat or running water or television," Winona recalled about the ranch. "We had to use our imagination a lot to play games. We were surrounded by books. I was never bored."

Leary called the area "one of the most successful, upscale hippie communes in the country." It was on the ranch that Winona developed friends for the first time, friends with names like Tatonka, Gulliver, and Rio. They would build hammocks and have contests rating their comfort. Or they would sit around and make up stories and play childhood fantasy games.

Her father commuted to work in the city and the older children went to a school almost an hour's drive away. Winona began hitching rides with her dad into San Francisco when she turned twelve years old so she could attend the Amnesty International meetings.

Hers was a stable and secure upbringing. "My parents had very strong values and still do," Winona said recently. "I just spent last week with them in San Francisco and they're still doing those things that got them labeled hippies. There's an eighty-three-year-old woman in San Francisco who's been taking marijuana brownies to AIDS patients because it increases their appetite and relieves their pain. She got arrested and she's serving time, so my parents have been helping her. I think that's very responsible."

Her parents remain her best friends. "They're great people to hang around [with]. They're both incredibly smart and intellectual and they could have become

very wealthy, but they struggled to pay the bills and stuck to what they want. That has to do with how I make my decisions. If they taught me anything, it's to trust myself and go with what my gut tells me. When I ask too many people for advice, that's when I get confused. . . .

"We had this relationship while I was growing up where I could talk to them about things that most kids can't talk to their parents about, like I'd ask, 'What's acid like? Everybody is taking acid in my school,' " Winona confessed. "They would say the bad side and would say, 'If you take it and go to a concert you are going to get a panic attack and freak out. If you get it on the streets, they make bad synthetic stuff that's just going to like freak you out.' So, I'd lose interest."

A stay at the Betty Ford Clinic or some other rehab is not in Winona's future. "My parents know what it's like to, like, take a drug and go out in public and flip out," said Winona. "They always said, 'If you ever want to do anything, you just have to tell us about it, and you have to go through it with us.' "

Winona always had a book in her hand. On the ranch, without electricity, she had to read by kerosene lamp. She read *To Kill a Mockingbird* when she was only ten and then sat down and wrote a short story about a black man being killed, telling the tale from the sister's point of view. Then she discovered author J. D. Salinger and her life changed.

Winona doesn't take her clothes off in films, but she has been known to tease a bit in photo shoots. PHOTO COURTESY OF MOVIE STAR NEWS.

"You know how some people rub crystals together when they get paranoid? This is my crystal," said Winona cradling her dog-eared paperback copy of *Catcher in the Rye*. "Me and [the book's main character] Holden Caulfield are like this team. I really related to the line that says, 'The goddamn movies can ruin you.' I'm not kidding."

The first time she read it, she didn't get it. She said she sees herself as skinny, but in a way Holden would say of his kid sister, Phoebe, "roller-skate skinny." She said she read and reread *Catcher* when she was on the road. Why? "It is a very comforting thing that I can go to, especially when I'm traveling. When I'm away from home, I like to read it. I don't want to sound too weird about it."

Unlike the character of Holden, however, Winona loves movies. Like Holden, Winona hates the word *genius*, "a word, by the way, that I don't toss around, and I know a lot of actors do," she said. "It's an overused word, and it should only be used for people who really are that."

Winona wrote Salinger a fan letter, and since she had talked about him many times in interviews, he already knew of her attraction to his work. "I mean, what do you say to him, really? I kind of said, um, that I, uh—just how much it meant to me, and thanked him for it." She later said she never mailed the letter.

When she was eleven years old, Winona sneaked backstage at a Pretenders concert and a security guard lunged for her, but singer Chrissy Hynde took her by the hand and while performing on stage serenaded her during the song "2,000 Miles."

She dressed like a boy in seventh grade. One of her characteristic outfits might be green tweed knickers with a double-breasted jacket, a green tweed tie, argyle socks, and loafers. She cut her hair short, so she was androgynous before it was fashionable.

It was her third day at her new junior high school in Petaluma when she was approached by redneck suburban ruffians while she was standing at her locker. She smiled when one of the bullies yelled, "Hey, faggot." She turned around and was mistaken for an effeminate boy. She was punched and knocked up against the locker.

"I got beat up a few times in school," she recalled. "Everyone thought I was a boy 'cause I had really short hair and dressed like a boy. A group of guys hit me in the stomach and banged my head into my locker, so I got stitches. They were calling me a faggot and I was like, 'But wait—I'm a girl!' They didn't believe me at first, but they felt bad when they found out the truth later."

She reacted to the childhood trauma in true Winona form. "I thought it was cool. I felt like a gangster. I got to wear a bandage on my head. I went home and looked at myself in the mirror, smoked a cigarette and thought, 'Yeah.' I was having such a bad time I had to get out and do something, and I thought acting class would put me around more interesting people. That's where I got discovered."

That's also how she discovered how to muster the strength and stamina to stand up to bullying directors and trust her own judgment about film projects.

She said, in retrospect, that "the bullies gave me my career." But her mother remembered a much messier story with a lot of angst and pain when she came home from school that day. When Noni tried going back to school the other girls treated her poorly, shunning her and staring her down. Her mother said, "Noni was so miserable and stubborn. She went down on her knees and said, 'Mom, I'm not going back another day.' "

But she did eventually go back, and she made friends among the punk rock and funky clothes crowds.

She was cool, in an outsider kind of way, but she was also fearful. In her prepubescence, Winona begged her parents to put bars on her windows because a serial killer was on the loose and believed to be in northern California. That was before she even had a television set (the family didn't own one until she turned thirteen). She missed the structure that was lacking in her early childhood. As she became a teenager and started maturing as a woman, she didn't like some of the open nudity around the ranch or her house.

Her best friend through her teen years was Heather Bursch, a model, who despite her name was not at all like the evil, bitchy, self-centered Heathers in Winona's notable film. "I want to do the backpack thing, but first drive across the United States, rent a car and bring no money and no clothes and write really bad poetry [with Heather]," Winona said at the time. "Then we want to go to Europe and do it there. We also want to go to Africa. We want to go to college together. We want to end up in Trinity [College] in Ireland for the last two years, but the first two years we want to go somewhere in the United States."

Then her career took off and they never made those trips, but Heather and Winona remained fast friends. Meanwhile, Winona earned straight-A grades, but she rarely seemed challenged in school.

"I was not Miss Popularity," she said. "Me and Heather were sort of the geeks. The other students would say, 'You're going to go nowhere.' It's funny. Now, she's in *Elle* magazine and I'm sure all those girls are feeling a little bit stupid."

The pair were a bit of trouble, too. Winona admitted, "In high school, me and Heather would get up in the middle of the night and raid my parents' liquor cabinet and go play basketball at the high school in the dark. It's so much fun—you don't know where the fucking ball's going! Sometimes we'd get up, watch *West Side Story*, then scale the school walls, get on top of the roof and do the Jets dances. We'd change around the letters on the scoreboard. We never had

If you look at this picture of Winona closely, you can see she's getting ready for something. There's a yearning here. It's as if she's waiting for someone to come through the door . . .
PHOTO COURTESY OF MOVIE STAR NEWS.

a very big word selection, but once we got it to say 'slut reek' when everybody showed up Monday morning."

After her parents moved to Petaluma, thirty-eight miles north of San Francisco, she enrolled in acting classes at San Francisco's prestigious American Conservatory Theatre.

"We weren't thinking of her being professional," said her mother. "We just wanted her to be happy, to be around more imaginative peers."

Winona said it was odd. "They'd give us these weirdo plays like *The Glass Menagerie* and I played Willie in *This Property Is Condemned* and there were always these twelve-year-old girls playing these women roles. So I asked if I could find my own monologue to perform. I read from J. D. Salinger's *Franny & Zooey*. I made it like she was sitting, talking to her boyfriend. I had a connection with Salinger-speak; the way she talked [in the story] made sense. It was the first time that I felt that feeling you get when you're acting—that sort of *yeah!* feeling."

Los Angeles talent scout and casting director Deborah Lucchesi dropped into her class and saw the diminutive actress's adaptation of her idol Salinger's monologue. Lucchesi submitted a screen test of Winona for the 1986 film *Desert Bloom*.

The young actress was supposed to play the role of Jon Voight's stepdaughter in the low-budget movie. The videotaped audition went well and it landed Winona an agent

with Triad Artists before she had done any professional work whatsoever, even before a meeting with her in person, which is almost unheard of in the entertainment business.

She didn't get the part; it went to Annabeth Gish (who later costarred in *Mystic Pizza*). One year later, director David Seltzer spotted her while casting Twentieth Century–Fox's film *Lucas*. Frustrated after watching seven actresses do the same scene, the director suddenly sat up and stared at the screen when he saw Winona's audition.

"There was Winona," he recalled, "this little frail bird. She had the kind of presence I had never seen, an inner life. Whatever message was being said by her mouth was being contradicted by the eyes."

Winona remembered walking home one day from school which she termed "like a hundred miles, the longest walk." She said, "I always carried my book bag with the strap around my head. So I walk in the house—I practically had whiplash —and my sister goes, 'Oh, you got the part in that movie.' It was really cool."

Lucas was released with little fanfare in 1986 though it became a video store cult classic. It was an excellent start of a career to be part of a film that deals honestly with growing up and young teen love.

Winona noted at the time that she got her start at the same age as Judy Garland when she made her screen debut in *Pigskin Parade* (1936). She was also a year younger than Elizabeth Taylor in *National Velvet*

(1944), yet she never had to grow up onscreen like other actresses did, and was thought of as an "actress" rather than a "child actress" from the very beginning.

She was described in the press kit for *Lucas* as "fragile, with a certain poetic mystery." She said she is lucky for never having to do the "Hollywood thing—to move to L.A., to do commercials or sitcoms." And, she admitted, "That probably pisses people off. But I've worked really hard. I'm not going to apologize for not struggling."

It was during this time that her parents were struggling, though. Her father took over Flashback Books in Petaluma, which still is the country's most well known bookstore specializing in the 1960s counterculture and the Beat era. Then her parents wrote two scholarly books: *Moksha: Aldous Huxley's Writing on Psychedelics and the Visionary Experience,* published in 1977 and translated into five languages, and *Shaman Woman, Mainline Lady: Women's Writings on the Drug Experience* published in 1982.

"It's a great book," declared Winona. "It's about famous women writers like Louisa May Alcott and Edith Wharton who used opium or whatever while they were creating their masterpieces. It goes all the way from Cleopatra up to Patti Smith."

Winona has summed up her childhood as pretty happy. Very few parents may have been as liberal, psychedelic, intellectual, and bohemian as hers were and few children lived in a house that looked like a museum

for the 1960s. But then, very few parents of her peers ever stayed together.

"My mom and dad are still very much in love. My mom is very sentimental and sensitive—she even cries at Hallmark commercials—and I've never met a single person who doesn't love her. She is completely non–judgmental. My house was always the community house, the one where all my friends wanted to hang out," Winona remembered.

"My dad is very intellectual and loving and he's so proud of me it's funny. He has a clipping service and scrapbooks and follows things I don't even follow. He knows every magazine and newspaper that's ever mentioned me."

Despite her quickly burgeoning fame, her parents hesitated at the beginning. "My parents really didn't want me to be an actress at first," Winona recalled. "They were afraid that I was too young. That it would take me away from home. But I told them that I had to act and eventually they realized that I really wanted to do it."

Her father recognized his daughter "had a flair for the dramatic, even as a young child." Her parents were cautious and wary yet supportive and they helped guide her at first to the right sorts of roles, always letting her have the ultimate choice.

"My parents were never really stage parents in that awful sense," giggled Winona. "They didn't involve themselves that much. They were always with me on location, but

Few actresses can look so different from moment to moment. PHOTO COURTESY OF MOVIE STAR NEWS.

Influences

*What makes Winona Ryder tick?
Here are her favorite books, stars, films,
and personal heroes, culled from more
than fifty magazines and interviews.*

WRITERS

J. D. Salinger
Truman Capote
F. Scott Fitzgerald
George Orwell
Hunter S. Thompson
Jane Austen
E. M. Forster
Jack Kerouac
Oscar Wilde

BOOKS

Catcher in the Rye ("My bible, I've read
   it more than fifty times.")
Huckleberry Finn ("And he's a great
   role model.")
Lord of the Flies
Crime and Punishment ("Man, that
   dude was really fucked up.")

PEOPLE

Her parents
Timothy Leary
Allen Ginsberg

CLASSIC ACTORS

Laurence Olivier
William Holden

MODERN ACTORS

Al Pacino
Sean Penn
Robert De Niro
Richard E. Grant

CLASSIC ACTRESSES

Greer Garson
Bette Davis
Maureen O'Hara
Ingrid Bergman
Greta Garbo
Ginger Rogers
Natalie Wood ("I have this weird
   affinity with her.")
Barbara Stanwyck
Patricia Neal
Jessica Tandy
Audrey Hepburn

MODERN ACTRESSES

Jodie Foster

Julia Roberts ("She's really hot. She gets to do whatever she wants. I'd rather be losing parts to her than to some idiot.")

Uma Thurman

Anne Bancroft

Sarah Miles

Joanne Woodward

MUSIC

Cocteau Twins

The Replacements

Tom Waits

Mojo Nixon

Debbie Gibson

Long before Dave Pirner, Winona was a rock 'n' roller. PHOTO COURTESY OF MOVIE STAR NEWS.

TEN MOVIES SHE WOULD TAKE TO ANOTHER PLANET

A Face in the Crowd

To Kill a Mockingbird

Opening Night

The Tempest, or any John Cassavetes movie

Picnic at Hanging Rock

Gallipoli

Don't Look Now

Walkabout ("I love Nicolas Roeg.")

West Side Story

Random Harvest ("The first film that had an impact on me, and it was from 1942.")

OTHER BIG MOVIE INFLUENCES

Something Wild

Mary Ann

The Stripper

Ryan's Daughter ("I really wanted to be an actress when I saw that.")

Withnail and I

Brazil

My Life as a Dog

Prime Suspect (the British television series)

even then they didn't intrude. They were too starstruck to interfere. They would watch what was going on and who was there. It was almost embarrassing. But I was never on a location without one of them. The other one would have to stay home with the other kids."

Her parents even had a subtle influence on her stage name. When telephoned to ask how she'd like to have her name appear on the credits for *Lucas,* she thought about it and looked around the room and suggested "Ryder" because her father's Mitch Ryder album was playing in the background.

"I knew for a long time that I didn't want Winona Horowitz because if you go way back [in family history] that's even a made-up name," said Winona. "My grandparents came from Russia and they were meeting a family at Ellis Island and had to say they belonged to them, the Horowitzes. But my father and I were just going through the alphabet and thinking of every name—at one point we were thinking Huxley, because they just love Aldous Huxley, but it didn't sound right."

Winona doesn't really know Mitch Ryder's music, but said, "I just liked the way it went with my first name."

The press began noticing Winona Ryder and asked for her to pose for pictures. One ingenue pose was at a grand theater in downtown Los Angeles, the Orpheum movie palace. There, she posed herself and directed the cameramen, knowing exactly what she would look best in and how she should pose for the photographer.

"Because you're very tiny, you need something that's not cut too big, so it won't dwarf you," she told them.

Always taking responsibility for choosing her roles, Winona said, "I think it's so important. First of all, it's gratifying and you can respect yourself. You look at your work and think, I'm really proud of that. That's a great feeling. I've been offered those big films that are supposed to be smart career moves but if it's something that goes against my values or if it makes me ashamed, then why do it? There's nothing worse than a sense of shame or that you're generating something bad."

She could never be one of those ultra-cool actors who ooze so much attitude. "I don't think I'd be good at trashing dressing rooms. I'd be like 'Ouch!'" Winona exclaimed.

During this early period, when she gave her first interviews to the press, she would sit in a ball with her knees to her chest and head hanging down. She walked hunched over, slouching as if afraid of the world. She strolled around a lot with a hat reminiscent of her favorite character Holden from *Catcher in the Rye*—a plaid hunting cap with fur-lined earflaps.

Always aware of her family's life and how similar it was to *Little Women,* her dream was to someday play a role like that, she said in her very early interviews. She hated some of the earlier versions of the story, and knew that something better could be done with the book. She definitely didn't like the medieval politics of the 1933 George Cukor film of *Little Women,* of which Winona said, "Katharine Hepburn's Jo is great, but she ends up ironing a lot." She summed up the 1949 version, in glorious Technicolor, as "June Allyson, all smiles, plays Jo as Pollyanna."

To Winona, the book and film should have been made to make young girls feel comfortable and strong in a male-dominated world. Author Louisa May Alcott's father knew many famous people, and she was active in many causes of the day such as the temperance movement, the women's suffrage movement, the thwarted attempt to desegregate Bronson's school, and even transcendentalism. For four years Winona lived at the ranch without electricity, a place much like Alcott's Brook Farm. Winona thought the parallels were uncanny and knew that she was destined to play this role someday.

But first she had to meet producer Denise DiNovi who would see her through both *Heathers* and *Edward Scissorhands* before making *Little Women.*

When her family finally got a television in her early teen years, she was enthralled. Winona said, "I hate to admit that TV so fascinated me at first and it was not in a good way. It still has an effect on me. Last night we stared at it for hours, at nothing, and it's like we were stoned or something."

For that reason even at the young age of twelve, Winona decided that "TV was a bad career move. I thought TV was lame." That insight kept her career on a steady track, and still does.

"I've been really lucky," Winona said. "I can count on one hand the actors who have survived going through adolescence on screen. But growing up in the (San Francisco) Bay Area, I avoided the traps kids fell into in Hollywood. I've made a lot of movies, but I would make them during the summer. I stayed in public school. I didn't lead some kind of weird, sheltered movie-star life."

Leary, her godfather, mentor, and advisor in these early career years, summed it up, "I see Noni as one of the first members of a new generation. They are the Kids of the Summer of Love."

CHAPTER 1

Lucas Begat Ryder

"It would have been easy to cast someone who was a wallflower or ugly or self-absorbed, but because she's so appealing it's rather tragic."

—DIRECTOR DAVID SELTZER ABOUT CASTING WINONA IN *LUCAS*

*L*ucas (1986) was a painful growing experience for Winona in many ways. She turned thirteen; she got her first movie role. It was also when she got her first squeeze of the grinding and merciless Hollywood machine.

She shuttled to San Francisco for acting classes, and she suddenly grew an unabiding and unexplainable passion for all things Irish. She wanted to buy a castle in Ireland and write books or screenplays there. She at least wanted to visit the country. But her continuing and blossoming success prevented her from achieving those dreams in order for her to fulfill others.

She had been to auditions to Los Angeles, driving nine hours with her family because they couldn't afford the airfare. She turned down some terrible horror movie offers and cheesy teen films. Instead, her first film set the tone for the rest of her career.

Why Lucas would ever think of another girl is beyond us. PHOTO COURTESY OF MOVIE STAR NEWS.

Director David Seltzer (who had written the screenplay for *The Omen* (1976) and would go on to write and direct *Punchline* (1988) and many other successful features), went with Winona as his choice for the role of Rina and it was extremely different from how he first pictured her.

"Lucas (the lead character) has no feelings for her but she is beautiful, immensely open, whimsical, and vulnerable in a Disneyesque way," the director gushed about his new acting find. "There's something strangely magical about her and wistful and ultimately reflected in her performance."

Charlie Sheen was the film's beefcake star in *Lucas*. Kerri Green wants him, but it was Winona's career that would come out in the wash. PHOTO COURTESY OF PHOTOFEST.

Winona herself described the role as painful to perform, even painful for her to watch. "In the film, I have been painfully in love with Lucas for years and even though he doesn't feel the same way about her she'll go on loving him for years."

The filming took place over the summer of 1985 in Chicago and in Glen Ellyn, Illinois, just after Winona completed eighth grade. Her mother accompanied her on the set most of the time.

The rest of the cast never heard of this strange girl who was discovered at an acting school. She was to play a character with a name as equally strange as hers—Rina, the unrequited love of Lucas, played by teen heartthrob Corey Haim. He plays a fourteen-year-old genius who skipped ahead a few grades but is considered an outsider.

Charlie Sheen played a good-guy football team captain. The then-unknown Courtney Thorne-Smith played his girlfriend before she starred as Alison, the heartthrob of the nighttime TV soap, *Melrose Place*. Winona kept her boyish short hair in the film and her photograph is not in the studio's official press packet since she wasn't one of the stars.

Lucas

YEAR:
1986

STARRING:
*Corey Haim,
Kerri Green,
Charlie Sheen,
Winona Ryder*

BILLING:
Fifth billing

WRITTEN AND
DIRECTED BY:
David Seltzer

RATING: *PG-13*

RUNNING TIME:
104 minutes

WINONA'S
CHARACTER'S
NAME:
Rina

Though Rina is hopelessly in love with Lucas, like the real Winona she is no-nonsense about it. "Want to go to the movie tonight Lucas?" her character pushes.

In the film, Rina plays the clarinet and talks nonchalantly about the former band teacher who blew his head off after writing poetry to a dental hygienist who didn't pay any attention to him. Rina thinks there is something beautiful in that, and Winona probably did in real life, too.

Lucas falls in love with a new girl in town played by Kerri Green. The only problem is that Green's character Maggie is in love with Cappie (the football captain played by Sheen), a very popular big stud on campus and Lucas's only friend.

Film critic Roger Ebert, reviewing *Lucas* in the *Chicago Sun-Times*, wrote, "It is about a very smart kid who looks a little too short to be in high school, and when he is told that, he nods and solemnly explains that he is 'accelerated' . . . it would be tragic if this film would get lost in the shuffle of 'teenage movies.' This is a movie that is as pure and true to the adolescent experience as Truffaut's *The 400 Blows*. It is true because it assumes all of its characters are intelligent, and do not want to hurt one another, and will refuse to go along with the stupid, painful conformity of high school." Leonard Maltin, in his annual *Movie and Video Guide,* calls *Lucas*: "One of the few Hollywood films about young people in the '80s that doesn't paint its characters in shades of black and white only."

One would think that getting a movie deal perhaps would have helped her with her popularity in school but instead it back-fired. Winona transferred back to public school and she said, "The kids were jealous and they were hostile towards me."

The attitude of the other kids didn't matter. She matured in leaps and bounds, and there was no turning back. Her choice of her next film role was important she realized, even at that young age.

"After *Lucas,* people thought I'd be seduced by the teen queen image and want to become one," Winona said turning her

Songs Inspired by Winona

"Winona" was written and performed by Matthew Sweet on his 1990 album, *Girlfriend.* He never dated her, although he hoped the song would get him an introduction.

"Just Like Anyone" was written by her boyfriend David Pirner of the band Soul Asylum. It appears on the band's 1995 album, *Let Your Dim Light Shine.*

"Wynona's Big Brown Beaver" was a team writing effort by the band Primus, a three-piece rock group from California. It's a goofy, largely instrumental number that the band claims is a tribute to Winona and her pet. The purposeful incorrect spelling of her name, no doubt, was meant to avoid a lawsuit.

She's winsome, intense, and mysterious, all at once. PHOTO COURTESY OF MOVIE STAR NEWS.

nose up and feigning snobbery. "I don't physically look like a teen queen. I don't think I really appeal to that type of film-maker." Even at that time, she had other plans for her image.

"I would like to play a glamour girl because it would be a challenge. I don't have anything in common with them," Winona teased in one interview at the time. "Maybe I'll play a one-dimensional, contrived character and be in a lousy movie."

The teen love story of *Lucas* struck the hearts of moviegoers especially the shy, poetic adolescent that Winona played. She knew that while other actresses her age went on to star in cheesy productions where they wore little clothing, she wasn't heading in that direction. She wasn't even heading in

Those who received billing over Winona in *Lucas:* Kerri Green, Corey Haim, and Charlie Sheen.
PHOTO COURTESY OF PHOTOFEST.

the direction of some of her *Lucas* costars, which was decidedly down. Haim had a career stumble, falling into a much-publicized bout with drug addiction. Sheen only briefly got out of his B-list film roles and hit his own publicity disasters. Thorne-Smith never got out of television. Green would soon disappear into obscurity. Sheen's success in *Platoon* and *Wall Street* notwithstanding, in retrospect, Winona was the only one to truly thrive after *Lucas*.

"I don't have problems, maybe some of the others did," she said. "The most important thing is to have a sense of humor about everything, especially about movie stuff. You have to laugh. If you don't you're so bogus."

CHAPTER 2

A Solid Start With Square Dance

"I'm not the most up-to-date teen, I mean I just never had a crush on Rob Lowe like all the other girls did."

—WINONA ABOUT
SQUARE DANCE
COSTAR ROB LOWE

Gemma (Winona) comforts Rory (Rob Lowe). PHOTO COURTESY OF PHOTOFEST.

Winona's first movie encompassed major parts of her true nature. Her second movie also included much of her own personality, but this time her role required an accent.

Winona jumped at the challenge of playing the religiously righteous Southern farm girl in *Square Dance* (1987).

"I read the script a long time before (on the set of *Lucas*) and actually thought that the movie had already been made," Winona said. "I had loved the script and could see myself in the movie, so it was very very exciting to know I still had the chance to do it. I got my agent to push hard for it and then started coming down to San Francisco and Los Angeles for auditions."

Meanwhile, back at home, her mother made her watch old movies. Oh sure, it didn't take much arm twisting, and once again the influence of *Little Women* on

Winona's life came up. She once told a story of how her mother made her stay home to watch *Little Women* and threatened to ground her if she didn't stay home from school.

"She really gets intense about old movies," Winona summed up. "My mom loves old movies and we watch them together. Greer Garson is my idol."

During this period she thought that if she didn't make it as an actress, she would like to be a human rights lawyer, exclaiming, "I'm real interested in both."

She spent a short time on a trip throughout South America and then worked as a teen volunteer for the nuclear freeze movement; she was a particular opponent of the food irradiation that she learned a lot about while traveling in South America. The practice was in use there and in the United States, and she was concerned. Always an ultra-serious child, she also focused intensely on the political war going on in Northern Ireland, reading about it daily in the newspapers. She also obsessed about Natalie Wood, telling a friend, "I have this strange affinity with her."

Square Dance

YEAR:
1987

STARRING:
Jason Robards, Winona Ryder, Jane Alexander, Rob Lowe

BILLING:
Third billing

WRITTEN BY:
Alan Hines

DIRECTED BY:
Daniel Petrie

RATING: *PG-13*

RUNNING TIME:
112 minutes

WINONA'S CHARACTER'S NAME:
Gemma

Square Dance was produced by Michael Nesmith of The Monkees fame. The project was first known as *Home is Where the Heart Is* but that seemed too down-home a title for the project. However, some critics said the title the producers ultimately did pick, the folksy *Square Dance*, may have kept people from the film, too. (Leonard Maltin deemed it "a much too leisurely look at a Texas teenage girl's coming of age.") Hot-at-the-time star Rob Lowe, looking sexy and making audiences swoon, was to play perhaps his best role ever as a retarded man who falls in love with Winona. The actress was unimpressed with his stardom and simply said, "He is sweet, handsome, and helpful."

Filming took place in a desert town in Texas, during some intense heat. Winona's best friend Heather Bursch came to visit, and Winona was very thankful, saying, "It was nice seeing someone my own age. I was very lonely down there."

Her emotions eventually wore thin, especially in one scene with her mother played by Jane Alexander. "I got started

Somehow, they made Winona look goofy in this publicity shot from *Square Dance*. Even costar Rob Lowe doesn't look too thrilled. PHOTO BY ZADE ROSENTHAL, ISLAND PICTURES, © 1987.

crying and just couldn't stop. I had to learn how to conserve my energy."

She was getting more scenes in the film than any of her seasoned costars and the work was grueling for the young actress. (In on-set interviews, Winona seemed quite articulate, mature, and serious about being a good actress. At one interview she wore baggy khakis, a blue blazer, and a t-shirt that read: "What a Waste. Oh, the Humanity."

She still looked like a boy, but her on-screen persona matured in just one film. In a particularly poignant scene, her mother, played by Alexander, says to her, "You're going to be a woman soon, you've already got the knockers" and an embarrassed Winona looks down at her covered breasts.

She had to have her breasts strapped down for the role because she developed very suddenly and quickly during filming.

Wise Winona Witticisms

💜 "Why do these rich, famous actors do these horrible movies that aren't anything acting-wise? Don't they have enough money?"

💜 "In America now there's this sort of trendy thing happening because there's a resurgence of black comedy. Everything is trying to be so desperately dark and weird. It's all, 'Oh, and then they meet a drifter.'"

💜 "Actresses my age usually have labels. I don't because I didn't do the Molly Ringwald kind of parts. Audiences don't remember me as a prom queen. I never got put in any category except, maybe, 'She always plays the weird, dark roles' and what disappoints me is that so many young actors seem to be trying to be hot. They seem to have a desperation to be famous. I wonder why."

💜 "It's weird when I hear that term [glamorous] associated with me. This sounds so corny, but it's like I'm playing a character when I get to be glamorous. I can't take it seriously, because in real life I feel like a nimrod. But it's fun to do."

💜 "I need to keep changing and consuming in order to stay happy. Sometimes I think it's an outlet, sometimes the opposite. It fills me up and I don't know where to put it. I guess I sweat it out in my sleep or something. It's great concentrating so hard you feel your brain will explode. When I'm acting well, it's the most exhilarating experience. When I'm bad, it's miserable. I feel like I'm lying to people . . . and that I have to finish lying so that I—and they—can go home."

💜 "Some people think that: 'She never struggled.' So sue me, you know? What do they want? More and more lately, I deal with blatant jealousy. If I were jealous of someone, I wouldn't be blatant about it. People get so strange here."

💜 "I'm sure people assume I hate Julia Roberts, because she's really hot and gets to do whatever she wants workwise. I like Julia. I know her a little bit, and I think she's a really cool person. I think she's talented and I'd rather be losing parts to her than to some idiot."

30

❤ "Do I want people to come to the movie to forget about the real world and to escape or to confront what's really going on? We're up there for everyone to see and listen to and we can really influence people both on and off screen. A lot of us don't even think about that. We're just acting to do a job and to exercise our talent. I feel a pressure therefore and an obligation to do the right movies."

❤ "I have no interest in drugs. That stuff repels me. I have experimented with drugs and alcohol, like most kids my age. A couple of years ago, sure, I would do something. But I always would get sick from it, so I never did it any more. I haven't led this perfect little angel life, but I don't hurt my body. I'm really insecure about a lot of things, but not to the extent that I'll crawl into a bottle. That's depressing. I'm insecure in good ways—like 'Gee, does my hair look okay?' "

❤ "I'm starting to read scripts in which I'd be playing women in their twenties, and I've already found it's more difficult to find a good young woman role as opposed to a good teenager role."

❤ "I could probably have the perfect career if I sat down and talked to people and made decisions. I could have a road mapped out for me and things could be very simple. But who wants that? It would mean not doing things I really wanted to do. I've made mistakes and I'll make mistakes again, letting my enthusiasm get the better of me, but I just have to trust my instincts, y'know!"

❤ "Some little girl will come up to me and go, 'Omigod! Winona Ryder!' but I'm no better than the fucking soda parlor, you know what I'm saying! Most movie stars, especially the young ones, are just *fucked up* and they're what these kids are trying to copy, and it just bums me out."

❤ "Whenever I've had choices to make, I've known how to make them. I don't know if that comes from the sixties or if it comes from something else. But it's a wonderful thing to know."

❤ "Acting is very strange. I get insecure—I wonder if it's all a fluke. It's hard to keep your confidence up."

Winona hits the road in *Square Dance,* on her way to a better movie. PHOTO BY ZADE ROSENTHAL, ISLAND PICTURES, © 1987.

The role was a stretch for Winona, a down-home religious Southern Baptist girl who sings when cleaning house. Winona hated to sing, especially the country songs she had to sing in the film.

She blushed when discussing her work with Rob Lowe. They hardly had a kiss in the movie, but she did walk in on him when he was having sex in one scene. In the movie, townsfolk think she tried to "cut his thing off" with a pair of scissors, but he actually emasculated himself in the storyline. (This was all pre-Lorena Bobbitt, of course.)

Winona's character wears straight brown hair with dorky wide glasses. She speaks hick talk with her grandfather, played by Jason Robards, and calls him "Pop." She shuttles between her mother and her grandfather trying to find her place in the world.

One critic raved about Winona, saying, "She gives an extraordinary performance that matches the more seasoned actors. Her naturalness and instinctive behavior are remarkable. In her nascent beauty, you see the woman she has become."

The film was described in the press releases as a coming-of-age story about a Texas girl named Gemma (Winona) who leaves her grandfather's farm to live with her mother. For Winona, it could have been a coming-of-age story about herself.

Director Daniel Petrie had made other dramas like *The Betsy* (1978), action films like *Fort Apache, The Bronx* (1981), intimate family stories like *Raisin in the Sun* (1961), and emotionally demanding films such as *Sybill* (1976). Costars Jane Alexander and Jason Robards starred together in *All the President's Men* (1976). Alexander worked with Petrie in *The Betsy*, and also starred in *Kramer vs. Kramer* (1979) and *Testament* (1983), among others. Robards, the definitive character actor, also starred in *Tora! Tora! Tora* (1970), *The St. Valentine's Day Massacre* (1967), *Hurricane* (1979), and dozens of other films.

Rob Lowe received a Supporting Actor Golden Globe nomination for his change of pace role as Rory, Gemma's mentally retarded friend. Lowe later hit a career skid when an underaged girl accused him of having a sexual tryst with him, and a videotape of him naked in bed with said girl and another man caused a worldwide uproar.

Square Dance didn't help Winona's social status at school, either.

"When *Square Dance* came out I played this real dowdy, puberty-stricken little girl and people thought that was really me. It's a character, and kids don't really understand that and they started teasing me about it. It's really so asinine that I don't really relate to it. I just wanted to get out of school."

Winona did her junior and senior year on an independent study program where she essentially learned at home. She completed all her assignments at home and sent them to school.

"I'm very aware that my friends are going to school with other kids especially when I see movies about what people do in high school. I wish it was like that for me. But I don't consider it a great tragedy."

She was proud as she headed toward her high school graduation, bragging to people she had a perfect 4.0 grade point average.

When she graduated from high school, Winona finally moved and left home for an apartment in Los Angeles with her friend Heather. It caused some separation anxiety, but her parents knew it was all right.

"My parents trust me and know that I'm not going to do anything stupid," she said at the time. "I'm sure they worry a little bit, but I talk to them every day. I have good friends down here who really look after me. They're great people to hang out with, and they don't bring me down at all. So I have a certain amount of stability."

And back then, she still entertained notions of going to college. "I'm not going for a while. I'm not ready yet. I'm going to travel and work some more, and then I'm going to go."

Even then, she didn't believe it and she knew it probably would never happen.

She admitted, "Who knows if I'll stick to that plan?"

CHAPTER 3

Beetlejuice Lay in the Stars

"I myself am strange and unusual."

—WINONA'S LINE IN HER
SUICIDE NOTE AS THE
CHARACTER OF LYDIA

Tim Burton possessed a script with a bunch of wacky characters, obtuse parents, and nutty ghosts. He needed someone to ground the movie, bring it back down to earth. He found Winona Ryder.

It marked her first big notice with her first big role in 1988, when she dug up the gravely disturbing part of Lydia, a deadpan daughter who dressed all the time in funeral black in Burton's comic classic *Beetlejuice* (1988). The critics and the world were truly impressed with her in the sleeper horror/comedy success, and she was still only 16. The role of Lydia was deadly dark, morose death-obsessed; the melancholy teenager, allergic to the sun, and given to levitating and seeing ghosts.

Again, she got teased at school. Her classmates in Petaluma once again couldn't separate reality from her personality and taunted her mercilessly. She recalled, "These hick school kids thought I was a witch."

Winona curls up in a corner on the set of *Beetlejuice,* a movie that curiously matched her own sensibilities. She would return to supernatural movies, in one form or another, several times. PHOTO COURTESY OF MOVIE STAR NEWS.

But critics proclaimed: "No modern actress has her watchfulness, her fiery reticence, her gift of girlish blush and fluster. Nobody else even tries to monitor the intelligent, expectant heart beating in a virgin's breast."

Filming took place in East Corinth, Vermont, the small town which is terrorized by the ghost Beetlejuice.

"The part [of Lydia] wasn't Shakespeare or Joan of Arc, but a definite stretch for someone who instinctively moves closer to the light than the dark," Burton said. "Winona felt very uncomfortable in her clothes. She had a real identity crisis, but still exhibited a real power and total believability. That's what I counted on. I needed somebody to ground the movie so it wouldn't spring off into the stratosphere."

From the first scene, she captivates the camera even while wearing all black. She observes a spider wryly at the house and says, "Delia hates it. I could live here." Then, she writes in her journal—

another movie where she will carry a ubiquitous diary.

"My whole life is a dark room, one big dark room," Lydia laments. She wears a comical black hat with a veil at a family dinner of Cantonese food. She has incredibly dark circles under her eyes. She hates her very self-centered stepmother, played by Catherine O'Hara, who is about to have dinner guests over and who snaps to her stepdaughter, "All of these seven people have been in *Vanity Fair* except for you."

That year, Winona got interviewed by *Vanity Fair* and none of the others, none of them, were mentioned!

The movie dives into the teen's suicidal tendencies and at one point the Lydia character writes, "I am alone, I am utterly alone." She is duped into marrying the living comic corpse, Beetlejuice. She dances to calypso music and flies around the room with a dead football team. It's funny, scary, and campy.

Beetlejuice

YEAR:
1988

STARRING:
Alec Baldwin, Geena Davis, Michael Keaton, Catherine O'Hara, Winona Ryder, Robert Goulet, Dick Cavett, Susan Kellerman, Jeffrey Jones

BILLING:
Fifth billing

DIRECTED BY:
Tim Burton

PRODUCED BY:
Geffen Pictures/ Warner Brothers

RATING: *PG*

RUNNING TIME:
92 minutes

WINONA'S CHARACTER'S NAME: *Lydia*

The evil ghost Betelgeuse (Michael Keaton) persuades mortal Lydia Deetz (Winona) to marry him. This offbeat comedy gave both of their careers an unexpected boost. PHOTO COURTESY OF PHOTOFEST.

Film Goofs

✱ In *Beetlejuice* the continuity is off with interior decorator Otho's shoes when he is spraypainting the walls in the house. Sometimes his shoes are covered in paint, sometimes they're not, and sometimes they're different shoes altogether!

✱ In *Heathers* just before the students at the pep rally "hear" the explosion, the flash of light that cues them to turn around can be seen.

✱ In *Heathers,* the continuity is off when Winona as Veronica throws a burning drink out of a window into a trash can. Later, when she and Heather are outside by the burning trash can, there is no window anywhere near it.

✱ In the scene where Christian Slater as J.D. and Winona as Veronica are preparing a poison to kill Heather number 1 in *Heathers,* the poison bottle is shown from far away with its cap off, but the cap is mysteriously on when filmed close up.

✱ In another sloppy move in *Heathers,* a police officer drops his baton, but has it again while chasing J.D. and Veronica.

✱ In *Mermaids,* Cher complains that Astroturf is going to ruin baseball. The movie takes place in 1963; it wasn't until the carpeting of the Houston Astrodome was installed in 1966 that the name "Astroturf" emerged.

Winona's career could only take off after this major film. Consider her costars: Catherine O'Hara plays the evil stepmother who would later play the mom in *Home Alone* (1990). Michael Keaton's portrayal of the title character was deliciously over the top. He went on to do a wide range of roles from *Multiplicity* (1996), *Speechless* (1995), and *My Life* (1993), to the first two Batman movies, as well as *Pacific Heights* (1990), and *Clean and Sober* (1988)—always trying a different type of role.

Adam (Alec Baldwin) and Barbara (Geena Davis) are the quiet couple who drive off the bridge and kill themselves very much by accident. Davis went on to stardom after this film, particularly after the success of *Thelma & Louise* (1991), and Alec Baldwin went on to become the most famous of the Baldwin Brothers acting dynasty.

Glenn Shadix has a delicious role as the spiritualist Otho—he'll appear later with Winona in *Heathers*. The people beyond the dead are also hysterical. Patrice Camhi is the dead Receptionist; Cynthia Daly the Three-Fingered Typist; Douglas Turner is Char Man; Carmen Filpi the Messenger; Simmy Bow the Janitor; Gary Jochimsen as Dumb Football Player; Bob Pettersen as Dumb Football Player number 2; and Duane Davis as the Very Dumb Football Player.

The cast included a bizarre assortment of recognizable faces in cameos. Robert Goulet as Maxie Dean; Sylvia Sidney as the cigarette-smoking Juno; Dick Cavett as Bernard; Susan Kellerman as Grace; and the quirky music by Danny Elfman all made the

Winona Changes Her Mind

"The whole problem is that I'm still learning stuff about myself. If you're a normal person, who's not an actress, and you change your mind, then it's normal. It's part of life. But if I say something now and then I say somethng next year that totally contradicts it, then you're going to say, 'Oh, she's a hypocrite.' It's just hard to be normal and have opinions. Because the fact is, I'm not really that opinionated, and I always tried to be like it was because it sounded cooler if I was more opinionated. It made me sound really strong or something. But then I changed my mind all the time and I'd like get myself in all this trouble. Now, it's like, I basically am whatever mood I'm in. That's what people are going to have to settle for."

Winona takes off with *Beetlejuice.* PHOTO COURTESY OF PHOTOFEST.

movie a surprise hit. The production design by Robert W. Welch and costumes by Aggie Guerrard Rodgers presented a mood that hasn't been seen before in film—clean and dark, scary and funny, all simultaneously.

Michael McDowell cowrote *Beetlejuice* and lived in an apartment in Los Angeles above Winona for a time, the place where he would later co-write a screenplay with her. He said the innocence she exuded is "self-conscious" but genuine. He said, "She understands how she comes off. She has made a choice to be innocent, and that's not to suggest there's anything false about it. She's innocence through and through."

Winona has said she always respected children and teenagers for their freshness and candor and hoped to always portray that.

Director Burton knew from the outset that he'd be working again with Winona. He was extremely impressed with her self-possession. "There's a fine line between the excitement of doing some good work and taking care not to destroy yourself," he said. "Winona is smart. Winona is sensitive. She knows she has to protect herself more and take it a little easier. She realizes she's been pushing too hard."

Winona loved *Beetlejuice*. She loved the idea of a *Ghostbusters* movie in reverse. Her favorite quotes from the film include Lydia saying, "I myself am strange and unnatural" and Beetlejuice's line to her, "I'm the ghost with the most, babe."

Winona found a director she was tuned in with and she liked that feeling. She said, "He [Burton] just has to make a noise and I understand him. His ambition is very humble, very internal. Most people, like the great big people, they have to compromise certain things to get it on the screen. He does his exact vision."

Burton talked about Winona's "method not done too mad," and how she bought strange, Edward Gorey-like dolls for the dead-pan, death-obsessed Lydia. She got into the role and she wore an ID bracelet inscribed with her character's name. She later did the same thing for future roles, wearing the name of each character.

"In *Beetlejuice* those were all my own clothes," Winona recalled. "I certainly looked and was considered weird, and I've always identified with the darker roles."

Little did she know, the crystal ball saw many more such roles in her future.

CHAPTER 4

Stuck in 1969

*"I was bored,
I was sixteen
and I really
wanted to get
out of town."*

—WINONA ABOUT WHY SHE
TOOK THE ROLE IN *1969*

The best thing about *1969* (1988), the movie, that could possibly be said was that it recaptured an era that Winona's parents may have seemed to be stuck in—an era who's spirit they hoped to recapture and never could—or at least an era Winona's family related to at some point because of the way they lived.

The next best thing that could be said about *1969* was that Winona developed a fast friendship with two of the rising stars of Hollywood, Robert Downey Jr., who played her brother, and Kiefer Sutherland, who played the man she falls in love with in the film. Their friendships live to this day, and she was involved with them during the public high and low points of their lives.

Unfortunately, despite some strong fan following, *1969* was considered one of the major low points of Winona's early career. Perhaps the best thing that the critics said about her was that she showed a nice flair for subtle

Winona has always worn hats well, even as far back as *1969*.
PHOTO COURTESY OF PHOTOFEST.

comedy, which audiences had yet to see at this point.

In *1969,* Winona once again plays the soul of the piece, the solid character, the narrator, and the storyteller.

During the filming, she revisited her real parents' old stomping grounds in Haight-Ashbury, but for the budding actress, both the visiting and the film were major disappointments.

It was the first time, Winona admitted, that she might have made a movie as a career move. She surmised, "I don't know if it was purely a career move, I mean, I wanted to work with Robert [Downey Jr.]. Who knows? I did *1969* because I was sixteen years old, I was really bored, and I wanted to work. And it was a big mistake."

Winona could tell while on the set that perhaps this wasn't going to be the big box office draw the director may have expected.

"I didn't do the movie because I thought it was going to be some good career move," she said much later. "To a true artist the career stuff shouldn't matter. But it matters to too many of those people who call themselves actors, but are really just posers. Some people are in this just

Winona flashes the peace sign in *1969,* a movie that was more notable for introducing her to a new friend, costar Robert Downey Jr. than anything else. PHOTO COURTESY OF PHOTOFEST.

because they want to be really rich and they want to have houses everywhere. And that's great. But just don't call yourself an artist and then try to tell everybody that."

She wanted to do a moving movie, and although she thought the Vietnam retro peacenik story might appear to be so at first, *1969* was not going to be what she had in mind. It was no Oliver Stone film. At the time this movie came out, she saw *Road House* on television. The 1948 film *noir* with Ida Lupino and Cornel Wilde had Lupino portraying the bitter enemy of a roadhouse owner played by Richard Widmark. Winona suddenly found something to aspire to, in order to give her hope.

"Now *that's* a film that is really powerful, it's a moving movie that I'd like to make," Winona said. "I'm thrilled if one of my movies is a hit. But you should do what hits you. If I'm in a movie and I'm not really into it, then I feel like I'm lying and like maybe other people will pick up on the fact that I'm lying."

Maybe she was too close to the war era coming-of-age storyline. Despite the appealingly good-looking cast, *1969* bombed badly.

1969

YEAR:
1988

STARRING:
Kiefer Sutherland, Robert Downey Jr., Winona Ryder, Bruce Dern, Mariette Hartley

WINONA BILLING:
Fifth billing

WRITTEN AND DIRECTED BY:
Ernest Thompson

RATING: *R*

RUNNING TIME:
93 minutes

WINONA'S CHARACTER'S NAME:
Beth Wells

However, Winona's friendship with Downey did change her approach to acting. She said, "Robert is the only young actor I know who's really helped me keep a sense of humor about everything. He reminds me to laugh at what I do, to remember that it's all a mirage. The most important advice I ever got was to trust your instincts and have a good time no matter what—not after a day's shooting but with everything you do. I'm going to stop doing this when I stop having fun, when it starts getting real serious."

Downey went on to get an Oscar nomination for his most fantastic portrayal as one of the funniest men in film history, Charlie Chaplin in the film *Chaplin* (1992). At the *Chaplin* premiere, Downey (a bit red-eyed from getting no sleep the night before) sat between über-directors Steven Spielberg and Sir Richard Attenborough. Kiefer Sutherland came to the show, as did Mel Gibson and Molly Ringwald. And off in the corner of the palatial theater in downtown Los Angeles, was Winona, standing for much of the night with her publicist and a manager.

After the screening, Downey pushed past a waiter, spilling a tray of salmon-mousse crackers. He ordered, "Out of the way, I have to get down the stairs." Downey croaked out an "Excuse me," but the guy was already halfway down the stairs grumbling, "What a schmuck!" Downey went directly to Winona to give her a hug. She congratulated him on what she knew would be a career-defining performance.

"Humility, that's what I've learned," said Downey. He also learned that from Winona. A year before, he was reacting angrily and arrogantly at the same waiters because he felt he was an important star with twenty films including *Soapdish* (1991), *Less Than Zero* (1987), *Air America* (1990), and *The Pick-up Artist* (1987). Through Winona he learned to grow away from the spoiled Brat Pack scene, and by his own admission, for the first time he said he felt like a real actor thanks to his association with her and the path he set on afterward, finding (for a time) a sense of humility and a lack of attitude.

"I enjoyed having her as a kid sister, I think I always will think of her that way," said Downey.

Men Who Loved Her From Afar OTHERS WHO ALWAYS PROFESSED LOVE FOR WINONA

❤ DIRECTOR/ACTOR BEN STILLER (*REALITY BITES*):

"Every guy I ever talk about her to admit they love her."

❤ ROBERT DOWNEY JR., HER *1969* COSTAR:

"She has this thing, I don't know what it is."

❤ DIRECTOR TIM BURTON, DIRECTOR, *BEETLEJUICE* AND *EDWARD SCIS-SORHANDS*: "She's magic."

❤ ANTHONY HOPKINS, HER COSTAR IN *BRAM STOKER'S DRACULA:*

"She was constantly asking me, 'Have you read this and have you read that?' I hadn't even heard of some of the books. She's enchanting."

A young woman who, perhaps, is wishing she didn't make the movie, *1969*. PHOTO COURTESY OF MOVIE STAR NEWS.

Paired with her other *1969* costar, Kiefer Sutherland. PHOTO COURTESY OF PHOTOFEST.

In *1969,* he played Ralph, whose best friend is Scott (Sutherland), both coming of age in a turbulent time in America's history. They take part in all the cliched Age of Aquarius activities like hitchhiking, experimenting with drugs, meeting nudists, and breaking into the U.S. Post Office to burn their draft cards. Their friendship is threatened when Ralph's sensitive younger sister, Beth, played by Winona, and Scott fall in love.

In the film, Sutherland's character makes a pact with himself. He is going to "get laid" before he turns draft age or he's going to "cut off his weenie" and he only has three months to do it. Along the way, Winona subtly seduces him, saying, "You are the most beautiful person I've ever known." They have a long kiss beneath a full moon during the first moon landing.

In one scene, while the friends are in college, Downey is looking through a telescope at girls who are walking through campus and when he spots one he says, "Looks like my sister. She looks like a cross between Kathryn Ross and my sister. Come here! Show her your weenie! Wait a minute, it *is* my sister!"

Later, Winona is named valedictorian of her senior high school class and says, "I would not want to go [i.e. to Vietnam] to die for something that makes people so bad." It's hard not to imagine Winona actually saying that from her heart.

She becomes a peace activist in the film, waving peace signs to soldiers in the back of a truck. She convinces Scott not to run away to Canada, but to stay at home and fight. At the end of the film, it says, "This film is dedicated to all of us dedicated to peace."

That obviously would include Winona and her family.

Winona said, "I didn't do the strategic, career-building thing, where I make two big movies, then a small independent one, then another big one. Some people really liked *1969*. I do the films I like. When I first read the script, I liked it."

Atlantic Monthly said she played "a brilliant, level-headed role" as Beth, but most of the reviews were scathing. Rita Kempley of the *Washington Post* wrote: "*1969* has rolled around again, but don't get out those love beads quite yet. This is a buffered acid flashback, a scattered, synthetic attempt at evoking sixties spirit with the Brat Pack sitting in for the flower people . . . an aimless drama, its purpose and promise [are] lost in a thicket of false endings and a fog of nostalgia."

After the bad reviews appeared (one paper called it "the rather tragic *1969*"), the nasty mean-spirited rumors began surfacing about affairs she allegedly had with her costars. She retorted, "Oh, yeah, there's all kinds of stuff out there! That the *1969* cast, Kiefer Sutherland and Robert Downey Jr., and I, are having a ménage à trois affair!"

It was her first experience with the gossip mill. "The first time I heard things about myself I was really hurt. People say, 'Just ignore it, or laugh it off.' It's hard, because I hear stuff about people and believe it. 'Ooh, really? She's a slut? Hoo!' So people are going to think it's true about me. And I'm sure I'm gonna be getting a lot more of it."

No truer words were ever spoken.

Robert Downey Jr., in a scene from *1969*, was one of Winona's closest friends during the early years of her career. PHOTO COURTESY OF PHOTOFEST.

CHAPTER 5

Friends Named Heather

"*My teen angst bullshit has a body count.*"

—WINONA'S FAVORITE LINE
OF ANY OF HER
CHARACTERS TO DATE

*W*hen she heard about the script—and all the three friends named Heather in the script—Winona knew she *had* to star in *Heathers* (1989). After all, her best friend was Heather, the model, and she had been missing her so much since Winona's career had skyrocketed.

And then, the lead male character was coincidentally named J.D. (as in her favorite author J. D. Salinger, although it was meant to symbolize James Dean, of course), and so she became obsessed. She *had* to have the part. As much as Winona hated to use the pretentious label, she called *Heathers* screenwriter Daniel Waters "a genius."

With this script, Waters purposely spoofed the 1976 schlock horror classic *Massacre at Central High,* starring Derrel Maury, Kimberly Beck, and Robert Carradine, about a new student at a Southern California high school who doesn't like how other students are terrorized by a gang, so

Her agent begged her not to make *Heathers*, telling Winona it would kill her career. Just sixteen, she stood her ground, insisting (without the gun) that she would make the movie anyway. PHOTO COURTESY OF MOVIE STAR NEWS.

51

he decides to off the gang members one by one in gruesome fashion.

She heard of the project during the filming of *Beetlejuice* and wanted to meet with first-time director Michael Lehmann. She wanted to emphasize to him how she took this story very personally.

"*Heathers* was showing how horrible society can be when a tragedy happens," Winona said. "I had a friend who killed himself in Petaluma High School and afterwards people were saying, 'Oh, he was so great.' People treated him like shit when he was alive. They never gave him the time of day. Then, I read the script for *Heathers* and it was perfect," Winona added.

"When you see all those sappy made-for-TV movies about teen suicide when you kill yourself and everyone's your best friend at the funeral, it's enough to make you jump in front of a bus. It's a fantasy for teenagers to get all that attention and it's dangerous. *Heathers* showed how screwed up that all was."

Her past director and mentor Tim Burton said, "She'll do movies that people

Heathers

YEAR:
1989

STARRING:
Winona Ryder,
Christian Slater,
Shannen Doherty,
Lisanne Falk,
Kim Walker

WINONA'S BILLING:
Top billing (her first)

WRITTEN BY:
Daniel Waters

DIRECTED BY:
Michael Lehmann

RATING:
R

RUNNING TIME:
102 minutes

WINONA'S CHARACTER'S NAME:
Veronica Sawyer

around her say she shouldn't do. She pursued *Heathers* on her own." In the past, the way for her to get what she wanted was to simply bat her eyes, Burton acknowledged. This time, it would take some work.

Winona remembered, "My agents were literally on their knees telling me my career was over if I made *Heathers*. My agents tried to 'strategize' my career by telling me I would have to do a big movie before they would let me do a small one and then I'd have to do several more big movies. It's so simple: You do what makes you proud. But people can't deal with simplicity here. They need things to be complicated."

Even Winona's parents did not want her to do the picture, and her agent argued that such a promising client should never gamble on a first-time director or such an edgy script.

Don't tell Winona what she can't do. She made the calls herself.

"I flipped out so much over the script, especially the character of Veronica Sawyer," Winona said, "I felt like if I don't do this movie I'll never be able to live with myself.

And I'll kill whoever does do it!"

And kill she might have. "The film is obviously exaggerated, but I think it rings true," she said. "And anyway, isn't that the whole concept of being a teenager? It's a time when everything in your life is exaggerated—every emotion, every event."

At first the film was to be titled *Lethal Attraction* and at one point the director renamed it *Westerburg High*. The first sounded too much like *Fatal Attraction* and the second sounded too much like a typical teen movie in the *Porky's* genre. The truth is that *Heathers* is a little of both.

"I read and reread the script a dozen times and kept thinking, 'I've got to play this.' It wasn't a question of wanting to or thinking I should, it was a case of nobody

Winona with her female *Heathers* costars: Kim Walker, Lisanne Falk, and Shannen Doherty.
PHOTO COURTESY OF PHOTOFEST.

Winona had her first serious romance with her *Heathers* costar Christian Slater. It lasted a few intense weeks. PHOTO COURTESY OF MOVIE STAR NEWS.

understands this like I do. Of course I wasn't so obnoxious as to go in and say that, but at the initial meeting we all knew we were on the same wavelength," Winona recalled.

Winona finally met with Lehmann. It was clear that she had a remarkable grasp of the role. It wasn't hard to convince any director she could do it after her riotous Wednesday Addams type role from *Beetlejuice.*

The 102-minute *Heathers* was produced by Cinemarque and New World Entertainment and no one there knew how to market the project at first. It's a black comedy, kind of surreal, mixed with teen angst, cliques, murder, and suicide. It has since become a certified cult classic.

Heathers is a dark satire about Veronica, a popular girl who runs around with three girlfriends named Heather, an elite and ruthless clique at Westerburg High. Winona's role as Veronica, a dark not-as-pretty girl in a club of three others is played as a calculating, sweet person with a cutting tongue.

The overly saccharine Doris Day song *Qué Será, Será* opened and closed the film, and became something Winona hummed to herself throughout the shoot.

At the beginning, Veronica writes in her diary (note the use of a diary again): "Heather told me if you want to fuck with the eagles you have to learn to fly."

Veronica is fed up with the way the girls treat people, and then she connects with the new bad boy in town, J.D. (which stands for Jason Dean) played in a very Jack Nicholson-like manner by Christian Slater.

Looking back on the filming, Winona loved the way J.D. comes onto the scene, sauntering and cool with his motorcycle and pierced ear.

The two of them begin killing their enemies (the Heathers) one by one in gruesome ways and making their murders appear to be suicides. Kim Walker is first. She plays Heather Chandler, who is poisoned and falls through a glass table. Winona gets to slap Shannen Doherty, the meanest Heather, Heather Duke. (Doherty, the brat that audiences loved to hate, would continue her superbrat status as Brenda Walsh on her stint on TV's *Beverly Hills, 90210.*) Perhaps to prepare for her role as the tormentor of Winona, Doherty would drive her new white Porsche to work and acted as a snob on the set. The third of the clique is Lisanne Falk as Heather McNamara.

Funnyman Glenn Shadix, who played Otho, the interior director in *Beetlejuice,* gets another juicy role as Father Ripper, who eulogizes the dead teens as they drop like flies. Lance Fenton as Kurt Kelly and Patrick Laborteaux as Ram play homophobic football players who are found dead in their underwear and are set up to look like they made a gay lover's suicide pact.

Carrie Lynn plays Martha Dunnstock/ Dumptruck who is the kind of geek Winona perhaps really was in school, and whose character befriends Winona in the end.

Renee Estevez as Betty Finn, Bess Meyer as a female stoner, Jennifer Rhodes as Veronica's mom and Bill Cort as Veronica's dad round out the strong roster of supporting cast members.

Veronica gets drawn in by the charismatic motorcycle boy J.D. who as a disaffected outsider listens to her complain, "Why can't my school be a nice place?" J.D. starts the campus clean-up campaign and the murders become almost fun, until J.D. cracks.

"No one knew the real me," Slater's character breaks down at one point. Winona turns to him and asks, "You do this before?" and later asks one of the best lines in the film: "Are we going to the prom or to hell?" Veronica initially goes along for the ride, helping plan a "Woodstock for the Nineties" in which the entire student body will be blown up. Ultimately, Veronica has to make a choice: to stand up for what she believes or to follow one leader or another for the rest of her life.

As happens in real life, when a tragedy such as a suicide strikes, the school in the film becomes a studied phenomenon attracting media overkill. In the script, the school is "glorified" by a hit record by a group called Big Fun and a song called "What Is This Thing Called Karma?"

Winona had top billing, which is rare in Hollywood for someone so young. The then-unknown Slater got second billing.

Winona and Christian made a good-looking couple in a movie that became a surprise hit both critically and commercially. There is still talk from time to time of making a sequel. PHOTO COURTESY OF PHOTOFEST.

Winona and Christian in a pivotal scene from *Heathers*. PHOTO COURTESY OF PHOTOFEST.

The movie catapulted most of the cast into the status of hot property.

Lehmann was a demanding director. "With Michael he knew what was up and if I started to get lazy, he'd whack me into shape pretty quickly," Winona said. But she loved the role of Veronica Sawyer, and grew into it fast.

"I'm still trying to get over my obsession with her," Winona said years later. "We're very similar, only she's quicker, she'd say things that I'd think of half an hour later. So now when I'm faced with any sort of decision I think, 'What would Veronica do?' And it's kind of screwing me up because the answers are usually something to do with killing somebody!"

At the time, *Heathers* was, in Winona's eyes, "the best thing I've ever done. Veronica was an anti-hero for me. I consider Veronica the part of a lifetime. I really love Veronica Sawyer, she's one of my role models."

The film was called "*The Breakfast Club* meets *Blue Velvet*" and the "definitive black comedy of Reagan-youth lust and greed." Winona watched it at least twenty times the first few years after it came out. The *Village Voice* even wrote a review specifically vindicating Winona's decision to do the picture.

For Winona, the film was a formative experience, she told one interviewer. "I was sixteen when I made it, going through this whole thing where I Wanted to Be Taken Seriously. I was sick of being treated like a kid. Then working with these people I was suddenly being treated as an equal and they wanted to hear my input."

She often found herself defending the film, even today. "I don't think we make that stuff [suicides and death] look romantic at all. We make it look sad. When kids die in our movie, everyone suddenly claims they were your best friend. What's romantic about that?" Winona got defensive when the movie was criticized for spoofing suicides. "We weren't parodying suicide at all. We were parodying what society makes of issues like that. It's like we're winking at you with everything we're saying. Believe me I've had friends who have killed themselves and it's nothing to be made fun of."

Even her best friend sort of freaked about the film. "I know this stuff scares people. My best friend, Heather, was completely disturbed by it, and we usually agree on everything. But I think the movie's very smart. It's the first time I've done a film I could say was really important. Even if you don't like it, you have to admit it opens a whole new can of worms."

Winona's first widespread media attention made her grow uncomfortable with talking about herself. "Most interviews of actresses that I read make me want to throw up. I read one not too long ago in which the actress actually said, 'I really, really want to play a blind person.' "

But Winona couldn't shirk the media attention. *Rolling Stone* named her the Hot Actress of 1989 which only increased the pressure. "There's all sorts of pressures on me at every point. But I just ignore strategy and advice in general because I can't listen to anybody but myself. So as a result I've ended up turning down a lot of stuff and I don't regret it," Winona mused. "Sometimes people would tell me: 'Oh, you have to do this. This picture is going to be really, really huge.' And maybe it was huge, but I'm not going to do anything for that reason."

It was during *Heathers* that Winona also teamed up with a woman who fulfilled many of her dreams, producer Denise DiNovi.

"She can play the unsympathetic or ambivalent part and audiences hang in there with her," said DiNovi, who went on to produce *Edward Scissorhands* and *Little Women*. "I tease her that she's like a little witch. Her instincts are so good it's almost creepy. From her first film to her last, you look at her and say, 'There's a movie star.' "

Heathers became a long-term success. Some arthouse theaters already had a *Heathers* cult following in 1989 that was much like that for *The Rocky Horror Picture Show*. Audiences shouted dialogue from the movie at the screen like: "Fuck me gently with a chainsaw" and "I love my dead gay son!"

A short clip from *Heathers* featuring Winona and the other Heathers, was also shown in the acclaimed 1995 documentary *The Celluloid Closet,* narrated by Lily Tomlin. The clip was used to show how the young women were obviously attracted to each other in the movie. (*The Celluloid*

Closet is a documentary of gay and lesbian depictions in film.)

Even *Tiny Toon Adventures* from Warner Bros. spoofed *Heathers* in 1992 with an episode called "How I Spent My Vacation."

The movie also left its mark on Winona. The script "was the closest I've been to anything since *The Catcher in the Rye*. During the shoot, I matured a lot. Before, I'd sometimes try to see how lazy I could get. Also, I think I actually became a little more feminine. Before, I just dressed however. I'd go to the set in my pajamas. Finally (*Heathers*) taught me a lot about what I want to do with my life, my career."

It didn't come without pain, she kidded. "My biggest sacrifice [in the film] was when I had to put acrylic fingernails on for *Heathers* and my real nails got burned through. I guess my fingernails are my biggest and only sacrifice for my art."

Christian Slater, only 18 at the time, deliberately played a young Jack Nicholson that sparked his own following. After his success in *The Name of the Rose* (1986), star-ring Sean Connery, Slater was also swamped with scripts.

Winona and Christian toured schools talking about the film. She enjoyed the experience. "It was free, and collaborative. We thought we were going to do nothing but *Heathers* sequels for the rest of our lives, that we could stay out of all the Hollywood stuff. The irony is that we're now actually living through the things we were mocking—the kinds of scandals."

Winona started dating Slater. It was intense for a while, but it didn't last very long. Winona and Christian were two major paparazzi magnets. "We talked about how we were going to do all the Hollywood marriage things like stage fights in restaurants, be really reclusive but then leak out everything; he'd cover my face when photographers came, like Sean and Madonna," Winona said.

On a talk show, Slater proposed to her on the air and Winona suddenly tired of the joke. "People have been calling me. It doesn't

> *"Noni was offered 9,000 light-comedy, feel-good, hits-of-the-summer movies and she chose one where she kills all her friends. She's a pure-at-heart person who knows that the darkness is all around her. She brings to light that there is truth and love even in the darkest impulses."*
>
> —ROBERT DOWNEY JR., FRIEND AND *1969* COSTAR, ON WINONA IN *HEATHERS.*

Winona Ryder as high school junior, Veronica Sawyer. Can we transfer? PHOTO COURTESY OF PHOTOFEST.

sound too good. Marriage would be fun, but I don't think I'm ready for it yet."

The truth? Slater fell big-time for Winona, but he was dating their first "murder victim," actress Kim Walker. They had already been dating a couple of years by the time *Heathers* started shooting.

Winona claimed, "We never fooled around or anything during the movie, but after the filming, we started dating for a couple of weeks," Winona smiled. "It was too weird. You know, when you're really good friends with somebody? It's hard when you try to make something work. It's bogus. It should just happen naturally."

Not much happened naturally for Winona during this time period. She still had her plans, still a love for Ireland. The longest relationship she had ended after six months because she was always away on movie shoots.

"I haven't been remembering my dreams," Winona said, somewhat disturbed about the revelation, "because I'm so stressed and not sleeping at all. It's awful. I always feel like if I ever stop writing, I might stop for good."

Her dreams at this time included playing a male role—maybe a Jet in *West Side Story*—or studying literature and history at Trinity College in Ireland, or just traveling with her best friend. She still had her sights set on visiting Ireland, but the more she discussed that dream, the more it fizzled. Then there were short-term goals like finding a dress to wear for her first Academy Awards ceremony, to which she would be accompanied by Slater. She considered borrowing her friend Heather's black sequined miniskirt, black high heels, and red lipstick.

But she actually seemed more concerned with the review in the *Village Voice* than with attending the Oscars. "Listen to what it says: 'Winona Ryder plays the conflicted Veronica with deeper-than-method conviction.' That's good, isn't it?" she asked an interviewer.

The limo waiting outside to whisk her to the Oscars honked and she screamed. "Oh, wait! Should I bring a jacket? Oh my God, should I bring a purse? What will I keep my lipstick in?" That's how she ended her interview with *Rolling Stone*, revealing another side of her odd self.

Qué será, será, just like in *Heathers,* whatever will be, will be.

CHAPTER 6

Great Balls of Energy

"I feel like a little doll in a dollhouse."

—WINONA SAYS ABOUT
HER MALE DIRECTOR
AND COSTARS WHILE
ON THE SET OF
GREAT BALLS OF FIRE!

Suddenly, just as she launched into the world of womanhood, the world focused on little Noni. "Oh please, I'm no heartthrob; I think of Shaun Cassidy when I hear that," she giggled.

Rolling Stone critic David Handelman wrote: "It's no accident that two hot young Hollywood directors, Tim Burton and Michael Lehmann, cast her as their voice of reason in the midst of cartoon chaos. She's wacky enough to get the joke of modern life, and savvy enough to be able to play against it."

She was called "the modern day Bugs Bunny" and she was the teen angst poster child. But, she was just seventeen.

"I don't like the responsibility of being a role model. What if I goof up?" She didn't hide her cigarette while giving interviews. She wore her characteristic baggy khakis. She just picked up presents for her *Heathers* friends at the

She shared the screen with Dennis Quaid in *Great Balls of Fire!* a biopic of rocker Jerry Lee Lewis.
PHOTO COURTESY OF MOVIE STAR NEWS.

Pasadena flea market at the Rose Bowl, a place she loves to go once a month. She bought a pocket watch for director Michael Lehmann, a silver belt for producer Denise DiNovi, and antique fairy-tale books for writer Daniel Waters. Men gave her the eye everywhere she walked.

In *Marquee* magazine, she told writer Nancy Mills her theory of the male. "Boys are more susceptible to seduction. They're wimps when it comes to that kind of stuff. They want it all, all of a sudden. I'm taking things slowly, thinking the same way I thought a couple of years before. But boys don't believe in gradual anything. A lot of them are clueless, the way they don't think

it could ever vanish once they have it all. They think they'll stay hot forever."

In interviews, Winona let herself loose during this period and talked freely about things she later regretted, saying things that would soon haunt her. She told people how she got drunk on half a beer, she talked about driving a rental car even though she was too young to drive it, she revealed that her parents have "the only library in the world exclusively devoted to the literature of mind-altering drugs," and related how her parents took the kids to splash around naked in waterfalls. She pined for Petaluma sometimes, but she knew there was no going back.

In this scene, the young Myra becomes totally enthralled by "The Killer." PHOTO BY BOB MARSHAK, ORION PICTURES, © 1989.

"For a long time, I was almost ashamed of being an actress. I felt like it was a shallow occupation. I'd go to see a band with friends from school, and people would be watching every move I made. They'd be judging me: 'Look at her shoes! I bet those cost four hundred dollars!' That affected me."

These days, Winona thought a lot about her roots. "I grew up with no money. My parents did what they were passionate about, and they didn't make money. And there were a lot of kids, so we lived with no electricity, no running water, and no heating, except for a stove."

Sometimes she exaggerated about her past, but she always talked about her parents' love. "Every week my dad would get a pint of Häagen Dazs, and that was our big, exciting reward. My parents compensated with amazing amounts of love and support, so I don't regret any of it. But my point is that when people look at me like I'm this really rich, pampered, privileged person—I am. I am

right now. But it wasn't always like that. Sometimes people think I was born on the screen and that I kind of walked into the world. Sometimes I'll meet people, and they'll be like 'Oh, I'm really sorry about my car. It's really dirty.' I mean, we had moss and mushrooms growing in our car. If we *had* a car."

Winona became unimpressed with her rising star peers. "I knew a lot of young actors who lived in these dumps. They have their books scattered and their mattress is on the floor and they're millionaires. That's fine. That's their way of living. But the reason they're doing it is that they're ashamed. And I've talked to them about it. You just want to say, 'Don't live this way to show people that you're real and you're deep.' It offends me, because I know what it's like to be in poverty, and it's not fun, and it's not romantic, and it's not cool."

The one person back home in Petaluma she kept in touch with was her pal Helene who used to hang

Great Balls of Fire!

YEAR:
1989

STARRING:
Dennis Quaid, Winona Ryder, and Alec Baldwin

BILLING:
Second billing

WRITTEN BY:
Jack Baran and Jim McBride (Based on the book by Myra Lewis with Murray Silver)

DIRECTED BY:
Jim McBride

RATING: *PG-13*

RUNNING TIME:
102 minutes

WINONA'S CHARACTER'S NAME:
Myra Gail Brown

out with her and Heather. "I'll think, 'God, it would be fun to be like Helene, being on the track team and going to the Valentine's dance and stuff like that.' But then I realized that I don't really have it in me to enjoy the social thing. I was always one of the geeks."

She made one relatively final and permanent move, from San Francisco to Los Angeles, even further away from her family. When she got to L.A., she tried the party scene, but it bored her fairly quickly.

"None of that is romantic or cool or appealing to me at all. I've gone to a couple of parties in L.A. to try to enjoy them, but it really scared me and grossed me out," she said. "I see star fuckers and people who do that stuff to be seen. It's kind of ugly. There are so many jaded kids now. I hate to see fourteen year olds with drinks in their hands chain smoking just to be trendy. It's like kids don't know how or what to do with all the money they suddenly have."

Her model pal Heather moved into an apartment with her, mostly to keep her company. "My best friend Heather lives with me out here—we've been friends since junior high school—and when we start buying into stuff, believing what people tell us, then we know it's time to get out of town. We'll drive into the desert, or just drive ten hours and get in touch with ourselves, y'know. We've taken some great road trips."

She finally got to take the road trips she always dreamed of with Heather, but it was as much *not* to go somewhere as as it was to escape from L.A.

"You can't hold a conversation here that doesn't have something to do with the film industry," Winona said rolling her eyes. "Every sentence that comes out of everybody's mouth is relevant to the movies. After a while you just want to talk about something else."

She was growing up, but the more she tried to make herself younger, the tougher it got. "I think of myself as a girl, not even a young woman," insisted Winona, while one headline asked, "Will stardom 'de-virginize' newcomer Winona Ryder?" But she was still a girl packing her handbags, socks, charm bracelets, Barbie Dolls, and *Twilight Zone* and Monty Python videotapes when she moved.

Then she did an interview with a reporter in Los Angeles and proved she couldn't even be self-revelatory and drive at the same time. The reporter wrote about how she almost got them in an accident.

"Insecure people don't fry my burger," she said deftly.

It was August 28, 1988 when the *Los Angeles Times* announced that Winona was cast as the child bride of Jerry Lee Lewis in the movie of his life story, *Great Balls of Fire!* (1989) and she seemed very secure about the choice.

She flew out to Memphis, Tennessee and said, "This role is a big challenge. Not only do I have to play a part, but I have an obligation to the real Myra. I can't let her down or else I'll feel really like shit."

The real Myra was invited to attend one of the screenings and when she began crying, Winona froze, saying: "I didn't know if she was crying because I was a bad actress or that it was so real. And then she turned to me and hugged me and said, 'You're a gift from God.' It was probably the most amazing feeling that I've ever had in connection with acting."

The hardest scene for Winona was the so-called "insertion scene," where she gets deflowered for the first time. She admitted, "Even in real life I'm not exactly a veteran in that area. I rented the *Big Easy* to see what a sex scene should be like and I got a little scared because they're not dealing with Ellen Barkin here. I mean, she's sex personified, and I'm not that."

In the middle of the filming of the scene the National Weather Service declared a tornado watch and that diffused things for a bit and the cast and crew scrambled to the basement. But eventually they had to do the scene.

"I have like a bra on and he [Dennis Quaid] pulls up my skirt. We're under the blanket and stuff and I'm thinking that this is really scary. It's about the deflowering of

Winona on Her Privacy, or the Lack Thereof

"For about four years I was really fighting that. I really hated that, and I still do, but now I've learned how to deal with it more. I'm getting a lot better at it. Before, I was really trying to rebel all the time, but it made [the media] more interested in me. Then, I'd give them something to tide them over for a while, and they'd just like want more. It's really like a catch-22. There's no way to win. If you complain about it, then you're spoiled. [mimicking a whining interviewer]: 'Well, then why are you an actress if you're not going to do interviews? I mean, it's part of the game.' But if you do them, then you're like raped! Then people are like writing lies about you. But now I do as few feature things as I can, and I try to make them as safe as I can. When they ask me something I don't want to answer, I say, 'Well, you have the right to ask me that, but I have the right not to answer it.' And I don't read the trash."

Great Balls of Fire! didn't do great balls of business at the box office, but Winona got great reviews. PHOTO BY BOB MARSHAK, ORION PICTURES, © 1989.

For Winona, her role was like a gift of cotton candy. PHOTO BY BOB MARSHAK, ORION PICTURES, © 1989.

Winona was utterly charming as Myra, establishing the childwoman persona that would follow her for many films to come. PHOTO BY BOB MARSHAK, ORION PICTURES, © 1989.

Great Balls of Fire! might have gone to the dogs if it hadn't been for Winona's breathtaking work. PHOTO BY BOB MARSHAK, ORION PICTURES, © 1989.

Myra and she starts out sort of meek and demure and then she starts into it and loses control. I started to cry."

The emotion worked great, but it was tough on the actress. "I've had a lot of propositions the past year. I know I'm ripe for the picking but I'm really naive about stuff like that; it's sort of creepy."

Jim McBride, the film's director, declared, "She is so charming and seductive she's impossible to resist. What can you say about someone you've fallen for in a totally sanitary way. She's very sexy without seeming to be somebody who has a lot of sexual experience. It's not as though she doesn't understand the kind of effect she has on a guy."

Nevertheless, on the set she looked incredibly young. She wore her hair up in a bun with ribbons, carrying a poodle and putting knitting needles in her hair and hugging a stuffed animal. Myra was a seventh-grader who became the third of Lewis's six wives.

Winona reteamed with Alec Baldwin—he would work with her a third time in *Looking for Richard*—who played the role of religious Bible-thumper Jimmy Swaggart, pre-scandal. She also befriended actor/musician Mojo Nixon and met the late Trey Wilson (who portrayed Elvis Presley's Svengali-like manager). He gave her advice she'd always remember: "No matter what you do in your life or career, work hard but always

Don't you just want to hug her? PHOTO BY BOB MARSHAK, ORION PICTURES, © 1989.

remember to have a good time, otherwise what are you doing it for?"

The story about the singer of "Whole Lotta Shakin' Goin' On" and other seminal rock classics ended on an upbeat note, despite the many downbeat facts of his life (i.e. murder, having sex with a minor, etc.).

Winona took the role because she knew she was a "magnet for really controversial roles" and although the role wasn't as risky as it could have been, she played four years younger than her actual age.

"I loved the role of Myra!" she said. She also liked the cast.

She got to know a lot of real-life rockers and begged new waver John Doe (who played Myra's father, J. W. Brown) for guitar lessons. He then helped her compose her first song about how her baseball hero, Steve Sax, left her beloved Dodgers for the New York Yankees, called "Fuck Steve Sax."

Winona cracked, "It was a love song— it was!—about how someone betrays someone. My next song was about actors who have bands that are bad, really bogus. I love to play, but I'm the worst musician ever. I'd never inflict my music on anyone."

The cult artist Nixon cast Winona in the video "Debbie Gibson Is Pregnant With My Two-Headed Love Child." It was during this time that Winona wrote a screenplay with *Beetlejuice* writer Michael McDowell. The screenplay has yet to be made into a film.

The *Great Balls of Fire!* director thought of Winona as an enigma. "She's got me

Obviously Jerry Lee felt exactly the same way.
PHOTO BY BOB MARSHAK, ORION PICTURES, © 1989.

totally bamboozled," said McBride. "She's just a kid, but she's been around the pool a couple of times, as we say out here. She's certainly not anywhere near as innocent as she seems. She was real nervous about the love scene for several days before shooting and indicated to me that she was very inexperienced in this area, and I had to sort of fill her in on things—verbally, that is. I took it all very gently and gingerly and tried to lead her there, but when we got to doing the scene, she leapt in with both feet and gave a very convincing performance. I'm not saying she's sexually experienced, I'm saying she's a good actress!"

When Winona watched the finished scene, she blushed. "I got really embarrassed. I realized it was going to be in the movie. The camera is on my face a lot, especially during the pain part. And then she starts to enjoy it, and that was the really embarrassing part. The face I chose is really revealing. I don't think I was very sexy."

She grew ill while filming; it was the beginning of a series of illnesses that struck her whenever she overworked.

"I was in Memphis doing *Great Balls of Fire!* I was sick. I was kind of delirious, and I remember doing the weirdest thing. I took a bunch of grapefruits. You know when you're sick, and you have a fever? You pick up an orange or a grapefruit, and they're comforting because they're cold, so you put them on your face? John Doe was playing my dad in the movie, and he brought over a bunch of grapefruits for vitamin C and stuff. So I put the grapefruits all over, like surrounding me in the bed. And I just laid there and tried to sleep." Her idea didn't quite work. "You get bored. I remember just panicking. And the digital clock was going: 3:30! 4:30! 5:30! I stayed up the whole night."

Winona's illness struck again when she fell to a seriously nasty flu during the last month of filming of *Great Balls of Fire!* in London.

"It was awful, I was on these penicillin-type drugs and I couldn't sleep or eat or anything. Finally they brought a doctor in to give me a shot and even he was freaked out. He thought the whole film depended on me surviving."

Winona winced when talking about it. "He had this horse needle and he was so nervous that he kept missing the veins on my arms. So finally he just jerked it out of my arm and without even telling me gave me a shot in the butt! My only vivid memory of London."

One of the things that bugged her when she was in London was the gossip. "I can't believe the rumors!" she screamed. "I'm going out with Dweezil Zappa. Alec Baldwin and I are getting married. Meg Ryan wants to kill me because Dennis Quaid and I are having an affair. And what's the other one?"

The director asked Winona to "act up." She resisted at first, complaining, "My style is more internal. I don't like watching actresses who think, I'm real cool because I have all these mannerisms. In *Great Balls Of Fire!* everybody was, like, way up here and I had to crank myself so at least I'd look like I was in the same movie as them! That was the 'biggest' I've ever been. I still watch that and go, 'Ugh.' "

The movie was a box office bomb, and she was proven correct once again. Journalist Steven Daly wrote that Winona "was the best thing about *Great Balls Of Fire!*" and that "the disastrous performance at the box office did nothing to tarnish the reputation of the film's female lead while male lead Dennis Quaid and director Jim McBride divided up the blame."

Winona didn't hide her disappointment with the film. Kim Masters interviewed Winona during this time for the *Los Angeles*

Times, writing, "Diminutive Winona Ryder, with her innocent brown eyes, may have one of the summer's most dicey roles."

Winona again confessed her hesitation about performing love scenes with thirty-four-year-old Dennis Quaid. "I look about eleven years old," Winona said. "My hair's back in a ponytail and I'm wearing these little Peter Pan-collar things. I was really concerned that people were going to see it and go, 'This is so perverted—thirty-four and seventeen.' I was afraid that it was going to take away from them watching the movie. When love comes on so strong there is no right or wrong."

Her once lofty travel goals became more concrete during this time period, and she still talked about attending college back east, but she was more obsessed about doing movies that counted. Her favorite movies of the day were *Brazil* (1985) and *My Life as a Dog* (1985) and she wanted to do roles like that.

Meanwhile, she enjoyed hanging out with Heather and wondered when fame would allow her privileges. "I'm not famous," she figured. "I don't know what I am. I'd love to be able to read a script and say, 'I want to do this' and have it happen—or call up a restaurant and say, 'I want dinner in an hour' and have them get me a table."

Little did she know, that such power was just around the corner.

The extraordinary thing about Winona's acting is that you never see her doing it. She is, as actors say, totally in the moment. PHOTO COURTESY OF PHOTOFEST.

CHAPTER 7

Cutting Up With Scissorhands

"Sometimes you can still catch me dancing in it."

—WINONA'S LAST LINE IN
EDWARD SCISSORHANDS

Some habits never die. Before she even started production for the film *Welcome Home, Roxy Carmichael* (1990), Winona ran out to buy a new ID bracelet with the name Dinky on it. She also told everyone who would listen about her dream trip with gal-pal Heather—they had taken many little road trips, but never the granddaddy of them all—the worldwide tour she'd been spouting off about for years.

"We've been planning for a long time," said Winona. "We were gonna do a Jack Kerouac *On the Road* thing. We're going to go across the country in a big boat, write really bad poetry. I want to get all that stuff out of the way so I won't resent college at all, like it's stealing my life away."

It was almost as if the more she talked about it, the more she was trying to convince herself it would happen. Heather's career took off too, and she went on a three-

Winona got showered with praise for her performance in *Edward Scissorhands*.

PHOTO COURESTY OF PHOTOFEST.

month job modeling in Asia. Winona's plans for a "mellow" trip and settling on the East Coast would never materialize. Now that school was well over for both of them, Winona reflected on how she hadn't attended a structured class since tenth grade. She decided she didn't miss out, especially since she was still living the life vicariously through Helene back home in Petaluma.

"My friend Helene, one of my real good friends from home, just had a prom. I've never had a prom. I've never even been asked to dance. She's picking out the dress for the prom. I was like, I want that so bad. Then I realized that maybe I've missed out on proms and keggers, but I have movies as my memories. I like what I've done, you know? I wish I could have had it both ways, but I couldn't, and I don't regret the choices I've made."

One of these choices was Jim Abrahams's new film, *Welcome Home, Roxy Carmichael.*

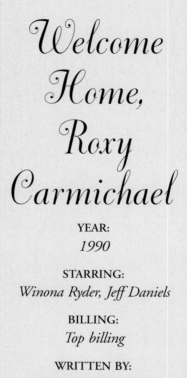

Welcome Home, Roxy Carmichael

YEAR:
1990

STARRING:
Winona Ryder, Jeff Daniels

BILLING:
Top billing

WRITTEN BY:
Karen Leigh Hopkins

DIRECTED BY:
Jim Abrahams

RATING: *PG-13*

RUNNING TIME:
98 minutes

WINONA'S CHARACTER'S NAME:
Dinky Bosetti

She liked the idea of all the animals she would work with in her new movie, including a goat and pig. (In this movie, Dave the Pig lives in an old boat and was "on his way to becoming a baloney sandwich." She says to the pig, "Don't be such a cliche, try to be a cut above.")

She also liked the idea of working with Jeff Daniels who has starred in such eclectic work as *Dumb and Dumber* (1994), *Terms of Endearment* (1983), *Speed* (1994), *Arachnophobia* (1990), and *Gettysburg* (1993). (His career is almost as diverse as Winona's!)

Winona plays Dinky Bosetti, who is a weird misfit girl in a small Ohio town. She's obsessed by the homecoming of a local heroine named Roxy Carmichael. It was a part written just for Winona by writer-producer Karen Leigh Hopkins. Dinky thinks Roxy is her long lost mother and hopes to run away with her when she arrives.

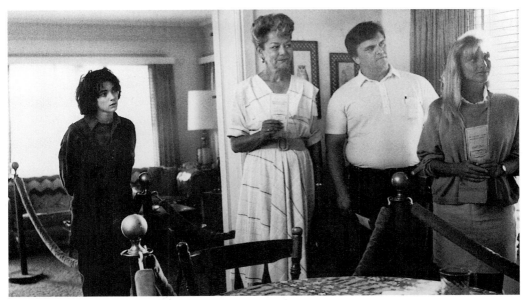

Dinky visits the Roxy Carmichael birthplace, standing apart, here, just as she stands apart as something special in this movie. PHOTO COURTESY OF PHOTOFEST.

It's been a great boon to Winona that she's been able to work, very consistently, with accomplished actors like her costar in *Roxy Carmichael*, Jeff Daniels. PHOTO BY GALE ADLER, PARAMOUNT PICTURES, © 1990.

There's no mistaking what movie this shot is from. PHOTO COURTESY OF MOVIE STAR NEWS.

In the film she has wild short hair and black circles under her eyes that are reminiscent of past roles. Her boyfriend Gerald is played by blond-haired Thomas Wilson Brown. The young couple eat junk food together and in one scene she kisses him with a mouthful of chocolate syrup. Kids tease her in the film by saying things like, "When are you going back to the funny farm?"

There are some hokey lines. She asks her mom if her breasts would ever look like hers. Then, there's the line when she talks about her mother with disdain and says, "You know what she calls a penis? A hoo-hoo!"

Winona went to her familiar hang-out, the large flea market at the Pasadena Rose Bowl, shopping for props and some accessories for Dinky, buying things like old *National Geographic*s and circus posters, none of which is mentioned in the script, and none of which was likely to appear onscreen. She considered buying a doctor's bag, but decided, "No, she needs a backpack. This is too uncomfortable to carry, and Dinky's a very practical girl."

Despite all her preparation and planning, *Welcome Home, Roxy Carmichael* was another dud on Winona's resume, and another bump on an otherwise increasingly stellar career path. The film was disappointing to her personally and financially.

She always had Tim Burton to go home to, and she did. Burton wanted Winona desperately for *Edward Scissorhands* and was the one who originally introduced her to burgeoning superstar Johnny Depp. By the time Burton called about *Edward*, the couple was already a hot item. Burton cast Winona first, then decided on Depp.

"Working with Johnny turned out to be really great," she said almost mockingly. "I think we have pretty good chemistry. Almost like Tim and I."

Burton said the only reason he cast her is because he wanted to get Winona into a cheerleader outfit. He laughed, "Winona is, basically, a great actress. The role in *Edward Scissorhands* is tricky because she plays a suburban youth who doesn't have very much of an edge. Winona brings a weight

Edward Scissorhands

YEAR:
1990

STARRING:
Johnny Depp, Winona Ryder, Dianne Wiest, Alan Arkin, Anthony Michael Hall, and Vincent Price

BILLING:
Second

WRITTEN BY:
Caroline Thompson (based on a story by Tim Burton)

DIRECTED BY:
Tim Burton

RATING: *PG-13*

RUNNING TIME:
100 minutes

WINONA'S CHARACTER'S NAME:
Kim Boggs

and believability that isn't inherent in the role. But she does it very naturally. You don't see Winona working at it. Her process remains invisible. And acting that way requires a great deal of confidence."

She said Burton is the first director who didn't patronize her, which is why she agreed to work with him again. Burton always gushed about Winona, saying, "She's the best. She has something that you can't even talk about. She's a thread to movies stars throughout film history, with something magical in her skin, her eyes, her gravity that you can't verbalize."

"She grows to have a connection with Edward and eventually to love him," said Burton who collaborated on *Edward* with *Heathers* producer Denise DiNovi. "It's unlike any movie that's ever been made; it's just a completely original modern-day fairy tale. It's sort of timeless in many ways."

The long blond hair was Winona's idea in the modern Gothic Frankenstein-esque fairy tale story. The film is horror star Vincent Price's final appearance, portraying the mad scientist who dies before finishing his creation of a man who has shears for fingers. Award-winning Stan Winston did the special effects, including Edward's scissors hands.

A kindly Avon lady (Dianne Wiest) takes Edward in and he tries to fit into normal society. Just when Edward finds his niche, things fall apart as he falls in love with the Avon lady's daughter, perky cheerleader Kim (Winona), and incurs the wrath of Kim's jealous boyfriend. Depp received a Golden Globe Nomination for his performance as Edward.

Anthony Michael Hall from *The Breakfast Club* (1985) plays Kim's boyfriend who is jealous of the odd but oddly hip Edward. Danny Elfman created the haunting music.

The first time Depp, as Edward, looks at Winona is in a photograph; he is in love, and it doesn't look like acting. She takes her shirt off while he is watching from her waterbed, and she screams, causing him to puncture her bed with his hands. Edward had to endure three deep smooches watching Winona kiss another man.

Depp grew immediately to respect his costar. "It would have been easier to hate her character because of the negative way she treated Edward at first," said Depp. "Winona walked a fine line. She played it so that the audience knows that her's was the only honest reaction—that everyone else was treating him like a toy."

Edward Scissorhands was filmed mostly in Tampa, Florida; the city bored Winona. "We were staying in a golf resort," she explained, "and a posse of paparazzi lay in wait for us." A chase ensued. "It was one of the most horrible things I've ever seen in my life" recalled Burton. "They trapped Winona."

Burton hated that, especially since he depended on Winona to be the anchor for all the weird cartoonish stuff in his film. For months after the movie was released, the oddly designed bushes were on display down the center strip of Santa Monica Boulevard in West Hollywood. Johnny and Winona would head past them on their way to their local hangout bar, Barney's Beanery Roadhouse. That's where Winona wrote on the bathroom wall "Johnny 4-ever" and with that cue, Johnny wrote "Winona 4-ever" on the Men's bathroom wall, and then had it carved into his body.

Like the odd uncle that he is, Burton enjoyed seeing the couple together, like watching "timeless old movie stars," he proclaimed, and especially delighted in Winona, who would always "follow her own drummer."

Burton said, "I'll never worry about Winona. She'll always make the right choices." Apparently she had done so with *Scissorhands*; the quirky fantasy film hit it big at the box office.

Look who's come knocking. It's Johnny Depp as the title character in Tim Burton's hit film, *Edward Scissorhands.* PHOTO BY FIROOZ ZAHEDI, TWENTIETH CENTURY FOX, © 1990.

CHAPTER 8

Exercising Powerful Flippers

"Sometimes being the mother really stinks."

—CHER AS MRS. FLAX
IN *MERMAIDS*

Winona loved the book *Mermaids* by Patty Dann long before she ever heard about the script.

"Some people think it's about mother/daughter relationships," Winona summed. "Other people think it's about what happens when you don't have a father. I think it's about being a teenager and jumping from one obsession to the next and not being able to figure out who you really are and what you really think."

For the smoldering young actress, a family drama was necessary at this point in her life and in her career. "I really wanted to get into performing with what I would term 'a family drama,' although it's a pretty strange family. For a while there, I was always out on a limb. I was a rogue. A family renegade. I wanted something different."

But *Mermaids* (1990) almost never got made. Winona was brought in at the last minute to replace Emily Lloyd whose credits include *In Country* (1989) and *A River Runs*

Hiding in this scene from *Mermaids*, at the same time that she was hiding her relationship with Depp from the public. PHOTO BY KERRY HAYES, ORION PICTURES, © 1990.

83

Through It (1992). The simple reason was that Winona looked more like Cher's daughter than Lloyd did.

A picky costar, Cher also insisted on multiple rewrites and the two stars supposedly got rid of the first two directors from the outset. The first, Lasse Hallstrom, who directed the famous off-beat *My Life as a Dog* (1985) wanted to have the younger sister, played by Christina Ricci (who would go on to play Wednesday in the Addams Family films), commit suicide on screen. Cher balked at that plot twist and Frank Oz, the unassuming Muppet master responsible for *Little Shop of Horrors* (1986) and many other films, was hired but was unable to keep the peace. He didn't want it to be a comedy, which was against the instincts of both stars.

"The first week was horrible," Cher said. "Winona and I cried every night. It was just the worst experience of my life and it ruined a lot of my performance."

Mermaids

YEAR:
1990

STARRING:
Cher, Winona Ryder, Bob Hoskins, Michael Schoeffling, and Christina Ricci

BILLING:
Second

WRITTEN BY:
June Roberts (based on the novel by Patty Dann)

DIRECTED BY:
Richard Benjamin

RATING:
PG-13

RUNNING TIME:
111 minutes

WINONA'S CHARACTER'S NAME:
Charlotte Flax

Cher's classic line, never used, but said off camera, was: "It's a comedy, not fucking Chekhov."

Directors changed, but Cher, like any good mom, stayed in character and continued nagging Winona before each scene. It led to Winona's irritation, but also to respect for the Oscar-winning actress. Suddenly, the young actress realized what Cher was doing. "It was brilliant," said Winona. "It completely got me where I wanted to be."

Winona doesn't like to talk about her role in director Oz's dismissal but producer Patrick Palmer admitted, "Winona led to Frank's leaving as much as Cher did. I was surprised she articulated things so well."

Finally, actor-turned-director Richard Benjamin came in to take over the project and everyone's mood improved. They worked on the coldest December on record in Boston for up to fourteen hours a day without stopping.

Winona became fast friends with her costar mom. "Cher and I were instantly compatible. We just struck up, like, an instant friendship. We connected real well and I think it comes through in the film. She's very wise, but also very girlish; she taught me how to relax."

She had to pinch herself that she was hanging with the former Cherilyn Sarkisian, who, with Sonny Bono, sang "I Got You Babe," the three-million-copy bestselling song that her parents had played all the time. She and Cher fell into boy talk a lot. Cher urged Winona to move out of the hotel in Cambridge and into the same building in Boston where she was renting a place. She gave the young woman advice about men, exercise tips, career counseling, and good dieting. They went to the movies and they cried, and they went shopping; they saw *sex, lies, and videotape* together.

Cher would cook healthy dishes like a rhubarb meal and Winona pretended to like it. Then Winona tried taking Cher out on the town during homecoming weekend at Harvard. When they were mobbed by admirers, Cher said, "Noni, I'm going to kill you."

A family photo, if you will, from *Mermaids*, with Christina Ricci, Cher, and Bob Hoskins. PHOTO BY KERRY HAYES, ORION PICTURES, © 1990.

Winona said, "Let's go to a kegger!" Winona was teasing. "I don't smoke, I don't drink, I don't take drugs, I bite my fingernails."

Cher wasn't sure about her work as the promiscuous Mom in the film. "I don't think I'm good in this movie. That's a hard thing for me to say." The pressure was mounting for her and she felt it. (It was her first film since she won an Academy Award for 1987's *Moonstruck*.)

Once again, the film's focus comes from Winona's character. She narrates the film. In order to prepare for the role, Winona read about all the saints, wore a cross, and tried to pray, although she really didn't know how.

Winona depended a lot on Cher, more than most would ever know. "During the last half of the movie we worked every single day and since I had to do a lot of voice-overs, which are difficult to get just right, it was important for me to relax and keep from, you know, freaking out."

She dressed like a pilgrim through most of the film, and loved the comfortable clothes. Fifteen hundred costumes were made for the film. The Flax family's rowhouse was built specifically for the film to recreate 1963 Massachusetts.

They couldn't hide their relationship for very long. Here Winona and Depp were spotted in full grunge regalia. PHOTO BY RALPH DOMINGUEZ, GLOBE PHOTOS, INC.

Winona's deeply religious character is embarrassed by her very flirtatious mother and confused about her own sexual awakening.

"They have a rocky relationship, like lots of mothers and daughters, but eventually they discover some important conciliating things about each other," Winona said.

Although Winona never had the same upheavals with her mother, she said, "I've been through much of her same emotional territory, so I was able to draw on my own experiences to help create the character. For me, Charlotte was the most realistic part I've played to date."

Charlotte is a nun wannabe, but is Jewish and has a crush on the church caretaker played by the adorable Michael Schoeffling who also had roles in *Vision Quest* (1985), *Sylvester* (1985), and later in *Wild Hearts Can't Be Broken* (1991). In one scene Winona ad-libbed a secret lick of the actor's jacket, which becomes a sensual moment in the coming-of-age drama.

"Winona's sensors are so good that I use her as litmus paper," director Benjamin said. "She's incapable of faking and is full of little gifts. That [secret] moment could only come from a wild, lusting, teen brain."

Again the sex scene proved painfully embarrassing for Winona. She threatened,

> ## "She's a strong kid who can think for herself."
> —CHER

"I was ready to pull out an ax and hack people if they looked at me funny."

She played younger again than her real age; the nearly nineteen-year-old was playing age fifteen this time. "Being fifteen years old in the movie was a little hard," she said. "It's hard to erase knowledge about life. You have to give yourself a lobotomy. But I tend to work from the inside out. If I'm there in my head, what happens with my body just happens. I have no control."

Basically, she was pleased with the film. Others were pleased with her work, too. Winona received a Golden Globe Nomination for Best Supporting Actress in *Mermaids*. It was the third film without stopping for Winona, and her ninth film to date. The press started criticizing.

"When I was young, I was the sweetheart of the press. They loved me, but were kind of waiting for me to mess up. I had no skeletons in my closet, no major past to talk about. I wasn't with anyone and didn't fall into that Drew Barrymore drug syndrome."

Later, Cher begged Winona to dance (she did pretty poorly) in the video for Cher's number one single that came from the movie. "The Shoop Shoop Song (It's In His Kiss)." It played on MTV for half a year.

Cher knew about Johnny Depp's secret visits to the Boston hideaway she and

Meanwhile, back on the set of *Mermaids*, Winona was doing her best to make something out of this movie. PHOTO BY KERRY HAYES, ORION PICTURES, © 1990.

Winona shared. In essence, the singer-turned-actress knew Depp and Winona were an item before anyone else in the world knew, and she felt the need to play real-life mother to Winona. Cher warned Noni about Johnny from the beginning, predicting that he might hurt her. Don't get married right away," Cher said, pointing out she was married by age eighteen to Sonny, and that turned into a disaster.

Winona smiled, "I got the whole lecture. I also was just being introduced to the tabloids. Suddenly people are curious about things you wouldn't even tell your friends. She's [Cher] been through that her whole life so she taught me what I should take seriously and what I should let go."

Johnny said he tried to keep the courtship low-key from the beginning. He remembered, "There were a lot of long-distance phone calls. A lot of Ma Bell. Cher was a real rock for Winona, a pretty tough lady. I wouldn't want to go rounds with her."

Most importantly, Cher counseled the young actress to ease her work load and ignore threats from her agents, managers, and publicists. The long workdays in the cold wiped out Winona, who was susceptible to anemia and illness. She grew very weak on the set of *Mermaids* and the crew had to shoot around her when her illness—exacerbated by insomnia—plagued her, as it had since childhood when she would read algebra books to put herself to sleep.

It was at this time that she was offered her most important role, and caused the biggest public outcry in film casting history when she first accepted and then turned down the role as Al Pacino and Diane Keaton's daughter in Francis Ford Coppola's *Godfather III*. First, she accepted playing Michael Corleone's daughter very publicly, but in reality she felt pressured by advisors to do the role. Many people predicted career disaster, although some said it could have marked Winona's move into more mature roles, but the truth was that nervous exhaustion forced her to pull out of the picture.

Cher told her to ignore the doomsayers and that Coppola would understand. "Noni was fried, really fried," Cher remembered. "She's not a flake, but you can't wring that much out of a wet rag. She's just a little girl, not a superwoman. And you can't start a film on 'empty.' "

Winona flew to Rome anyway, but never left the hotel room. "I was sick with a respiratory infection and 104 degree fever," Winona said in retrospect. "I was told by the doctor that I couldn't work. Nobody believed it. The truth was so simple."

Before she gave up the role in Italy, Johnny stayed at her side. She had not slept

Winona and Cher became close during the making of *Mermaids*. They were close enough for Noni to ask Cher for advice about her relationship with Johnny Depp. PHOTO BY KERRY HAYES, ORION PICTURES, © 1990.

What Character Is Most Like Her

A rundown of her characters and how close they are to being like her.

LITTLE WOMEN

Role: Really a cross between Jo March and Jane Austen, with a lot of Winona thrown in.

Winona says: "I'm actually more like Jo in real life than any other character I think I've played. At least I'd like to think that."

Analysis: Even her friend and producer Denise DiNovi says the character is more like Winona than any other. Independent, sassy, her own woman; "Winona may be little, but her personality is big."

Likeness: 98 percent.

REALITY BITES

Role: A young documentary filmmaker looking for work who hangs out with slacker friends and who are all afraid of selling out.

Winona says: "It captures some parts of me, awkward, antisocial, but I wished I had the comebacks instantaneously like she did."

Analysis: Friends say it captures Winona's charming, funny, sweet aura more than any role. She put a lot of herself into it, and it represents the friends she has in real life.

Likeness: 96 percent.

HOW TO MAKE AN AMERICAN QUILT

Role: A young woman too careful about getting married, has an affair and turns to her older female relatives and friends for answers.

Winona says: "I liked this character as a person; I think we'd probably be friends."

Analysis: Considering her history with men and her skittishness about marriage, some of the lines about men and relationships are probably lines Winona used in real life. She also turns to older women and other actresses for advice.

Likeness: 91 percent.

HEATHERS

Role: A youth who is desperately trying to impress her friends in an elite social clique and finds herself sucked in by a bad-boy boyfriend.

Winona says: "I think Veronica Sawyer is a role model for me, I want to be like her."

Analysis: She's never been in a clique like that, nor would she ever. Yet, the real Winona is as impulsive, headstrong, driven, and calculating as Veronica— and she is drawn to bad boys like a moth to flame.

Likeness: 86 percent.

WELCOME HOME, ROXY CARMICHAEL

Role: A girl who loves animals, doesn't care what she looks like, and fantasizes about life.

Winona says: "She's a lot like me, sort of. She's like no other character I've come across in my life. She's very cool."

Analysis: She is headstrong and asks other people for advice, but relies on her own instincts anyway. She dresses a lot like Winona did in school.

Likeness: 83 percent.

BEETLEJUICE

Role: A dark and lonely misfit who is fascinated by death and spiders and has no friends except ghosts who are older than she is.

Winona says: "She was very lonely and withdrawn, and she let it be known through her style. I was very much a loner in school, too."

Analysis: Winona has had bouts with fascination about death, was sort of a geek in school, and always liked spiders.

Likeness: 79 percent.

MERMAIDS

Role: A Jewish girl who longs to be a nun, a virgin who can't get along with her promiscuous mother.

Winona says: "It's my most complex character to date, and the most realistic part I've had."

Analysis: Winona's not religious at all, perhaps is a virgin at this time, and really does get along well with her mother. Charlotte's quirky fast-talk, hesitating shyness, natural beauty, and sexual urgings are probably the parts of the character most like Winona.

Likeness: 72 percent.

BOYS

Role: An elite sophisticate snob who falls for a school boy.

Winona says: "I didn't quite get the role. I thought I did, but when I got there I realized I didn't."

Analysis: The way she treated these boys at first is probably how Winona treats obnoxious fans at first, otherwise there's little comparison.

Likeness: 36 percent.

AGE OF INNOCENCE

Role: A beautiful, sometimes naive fiancée, who loves to incessantly talk about other people's lives.

Winona says: "It's the first time I ever felt proud of myself as an actress. They kept telling me to downplay the role, make it less."

Analysis: Winona likes her share of gossip, but only if it isn't mean. In real life, though she'd have dumped Daniel Day-Lewis in a second after she wised up to his infatuations.

Likeness: 28 percent.

GREAT BALLS OF FIRE!

Role: An innocent thirteen-year-old marries her cousin and stays in an abusive relationship.

Winona says: "I loved that movie, but it was probably the furthest you could get from the real me. But the thing I associated with was her strength, her honesty, and her heart."

Analysis: Strength, honesty, purity, and beauty—but not as much as is portrayed on screen—is all that Winona has in common with her character.

Likeness: 19 percent.

It would've taken a net for Michael Schoeffling to catch Winona during her real-life romance with Johnny Depp. Thanks to the *Mermaids* script, he was cast as the man of her dreams.
PHOTO BY KERRY HAYES, ORION PICTURES, © 1990.

for four nights, and the sinus and bronchial infections kept her from going to costume fittings.

She was in no condition to work and she asked agent Andrew Eastman of ICM what to do. He told her she had to work. Johnny took care of her, ordering room service and—in a real-life recreation of what Winona did for Shannen Doherty's character in *Heathers*—stuck his finger down her throat to help her throw up and feel better.

Some people said she felt she was not quite right for the role, some speculated she was pregnant, or she had had a nervous breakdown, or Johnny talked her out of it because he wanted her to work with him. Winona's fever would not break and her respiratory virus worsened. The whole crew protested when Coppola finally cast his daughter Sofia in Winona's role. Sofia couldn't act and the film's credibility suffered, critics said.

After finally seeing the film, Winona said, "I think she [Sofia] did a wonderful job. I really like her a lot."

Winona flew home to Petaluma for a dose of mother care with chicken soup and herbal tea. Johnny wondered if they should openly talk about their budding romance. No, Noni said, not yet, not quite yet.

The sisterly relationship between young Ricci and Winona seemed particularly genuine on film.
PHOTO COURTESY OF PHOTOFEST.

CHAPTER 9

The Depp Depression

> "My relationship with Winona; it was my mistake to be as open as we were, but I thought if we were honest it would destroy that curiosity monster. Instead it fed; it gave people license to feel they were a part of it."

—JOHNNY DEPP ABOUT HIS
THREE YEARS WITH WINONA.

While it lasted, Winona and Depp were the prince and princess of Hollywood. After a fashion, they dressed for their parts. PHOTO BY RALPH DOMINGUEZ, GLOBE PHOTOS, INC.

For Winona, it was the best of times and it was the worst of times. At first, it seemed like a match made in heaven. Call it the U.S. version of Lady Di and Prince Charles—at least at the time—or the modern day Jack and Jackie, the Mary Pickford and Douglas Fairbanks public love affair, or the Ken and Barbie of Hollywood hip. From the moment they went public with their affections, everyone loved Johnny and Winona. And everyone watched through a magnifying glass.

Speculation that they were having an affair first ignited when Johnny flew in from Vancouver to Boston to spend the weekend with Winona on October 17, 1989 while she was filming *Mermaids*. Cher knew what was up; Winona talked to her about it and confided she could never get used to "the scene" around Johnny, who had teenage girls chasing him everywhere he went, after starring in TV's *21 Jump Street*, and especially after the film *Cry-Baby* (1990).

They first met at *The Great Balls of Fire!* premiere in 1989. Tim Burton made the introduction and predicted sparks would fly. He's eight years older than she is; he'd already been married once to actress Lori Anne Allison for two years and had been engaged to actresses Sheri- lyn Fenn and Jennifer Grey. She was dating fresh-faced Robert Sean Leonard from *Dead Poet's Society* (1989) who would later play her son in *The Age of Innocence* (1993).

"People assume it bothers me that he's been engaged before, but it really doesn't," Winona insisted at the time. "We have a connection on a deeper level. We have the same coloring but we're from very different backgrounds, so we're interested in each other the whole time."

The first incident of their PDA (public display of affection) was on January 25, 1990 in Las Vegas in front of two thousand people at the National Association of The- ater Owners at their convention called ShoWest. She was receiving the prestigious honor of being named Female Star of Tomorrow. She followed past recipients such as Kim Basinger, Jamie Lee Curtis, and Helen Slater. He was being named Male Star of Tomorrow. How appropriate.

When they won the honors earlier in the day—and all throughout the conference in fact—they were smooching and hugging and giggling together. This was no publicity stunt. At the ceremony, they surprised audi- ences when they fell to the floor in a groping embrace.

They officially became engaged on Feb- ruary 26, 1990 when the *Los Angeles Times* announced that Depp, 26, and Ryder, 18, made it official. A week later, it hit *Newsweek* that the *21 Jump Street* TV star would finally no longer be the world's most eligible bachelor, and *People* magazine announced that Winona bought a one mil- lion dollar home in Malibu and she would be the sole owner listed.

Johnny always carried old fashioned ideas about marriage, saying, "I want to get married and have kids. I want to be an old man with a beer belly sitting on a porch looking at a lake or something."

For the first time, Winona said to friends, "I want to get married and I've got that feeling that this is right." Some of their friends agreed.

"They're a couple for movie heaven," insisted Johnny's *Cry-Baby* director John Waters. "They're not after each other's money, they're both hot and their careers are equal."

US magazine even put together a Romance Report chart that had Winona linked sexually to Christian Slater, Julian Lennon, Adam Horovitz of the Beastie Boys, and distantly to Jack Nicholson, Clint Eastwood, and Madonna.

Before Johnny, despite her "publicity fling" with Slater, Winona hadn't had many boyfriends. She said herself that the biggest

Winona fell real hard for Depp; neither of them had to act their *Edward Scissorhands* love scenes.
PHOTO COURTESY OF PHOTOFEST.

On-Screen Boyfriends

Winona's boyfriends in the movies, and whatever became of them.

BOYFRIEND	MOVIE OUTCOME	REAL-LIFE SUCCESS
THE AGE OF INNOCENCE		
Daniel Day-Lewis	He courts her and marries her but loves another	He gets another chance in *The Crucible*
BEETLEJUICE		
Michael Keaton	Almost marries Winona	The former Batman is a *multiple* success [i.e. *Multiplicity*, 1996]
BOYS		
Lukas Haas	Nervous both on and off screen with her	Followed this movie by playing a gay hustler in *Johns*
BRAM STOKER'S DRACULA		
Gary Oldman	A few nasty kisses leaving teeth marks	He follows it by playing more murderous roles
Keanu Reeves	Kisses her a bit unemotionally	His career picks up *Speed* much later
EDWARD SCISSORHANDS		
Johnny Depp	Doesn't get girl in the end	Independent cult film superstar
Anthony Michael Hall	Jerk boyfriend, gets three deep smooches from her	No more kiss for this Hall
GREAT BALLS OF FIRE!		
Dennis Quaid	Marries her at thirteen	Ends up marrying Meg Ryan
HEATHERS		
Christian Slater	Flirts with her and kills her friends	Jack Nicholson's secret love child?

THE HOUSE OF THE SPIRITS

| Antonio Banderas | Has a brief scene in bed with her before she gets tortured | Becomes a superstar only after his sexy scene with Brad Pitt |

HOW TO MAKE AN AMERICAN QUILT

| Dermot Mulroney | Is engaged to marry her and gets her in the end | Finally has some decent roles coming up |
| Johnathon Schaech | Seduces Winona with a strawberry | *That Thing You Do!* The next Brad Pitt? |

LUCAS

| Corey Haim | A genius too dumb to see that Winona's in love with him | An actor too dumb to pick good film roles |

MERMAIDS

| Michael Schoeffling | The shy church caretaker | He's history after *Wild Hearts Can't Be Broken, Vision Quest,* and *Sylvester* |

1969

| Kiefer Sutherland | Kisses her during the moon landing | Plays some of the most villainous characters in screen history |

REALITY BITES

| Ethan Hawke | Afraid to sleep with her because it may jeopardize their friendship | A steady stream of good hits |

SQUARE DANCE

| Rob Lowe | He tries to cut his penis off when Winona catches him in bed with another woman | Hit an all-time career Lowe and a private video got released |

WELCOME HOME, ROXY CARMICHAEL

| Thomas Wilson Brown | Kisses Winona with lots of chocolate syrup | Has disappeared |

misconception about her during this time was that "I've been with a lot of guys in the Biblical sense, and that I've had a lot of boyfriends or experiences in that way." Not true. In fact, even after *Great Balls*, she said, "It's still kind of embarrassing to see yourself on screen kissing and being like that."

She felt her relationship with Johnny really reflected that of Kim and Edward's in *Edward Scissorhands*. "The reason she fell in love with Edward was because she felt different," Winona thought aloud. "She was trying to live this perfect, normal all-American teenager life, but she's not like that inside. That's what attracted me to the role in the first place. That inside she's really weird."

No wedding date was set for quite some time, but on February 25, 1991, Johnny gave Winona a diamond ring and the couple celebrated their first year together.

Then, in a much-publicized move, he drove to the Sunset Strip Tattoo Parlor and Johnny had a huge double banner "Winona Forever" tattooed on his right upper arm. His was the most photographed deltoid at the time. She refused to get a tattoo in response. But Winona was flattered. "I was thrilled when he got the tattoo. Wouldn't any woman be?"

At the time, they both owned separate homes in Los Angeles and despite Winona's new house in Malibu, they looked for one house they could live in together. They searched for about eighteen months but couldn't decide on anything. For tax purposes, they each kept their own homes.

"It means nothing, they can have two places to live," said their publicists, "and when they fight with each other, they have a place to go." But to others it already showed cracks in their relationship because they couldn't even commit to a single place to live. The photographers followed them everywhere. Youth and a kind heart doesn't keep one out of supermarket tabloids the shy couple soon discovered.

They were recognized wherever they went. The paparazzi can be a nightmare, and once Winona even saw a video camera pointed in their bedroom window when she woke up one morning.

"I don't really read those papers," Winona said. "You hear about it. It's like a mosquito; it's annoying, but you can't pay too much attention, because it's too tiresome. I don't even like discussing my relationship with Johnny with the press. It's nobody's business. How do you explain a relationship anyway? Nobody knows anything about it, nobody, not even friends know what my relationship is like. I don't even know it."

The pressure got too hot and the couple fled to New York to seek some anonymity. She flushed with both anger and embarrassment when catching a cab and seeing a bumper sticker in Manhattan that read: "Honk if you've never been engaged to Johnny Depp."

"I get very protective because people try to categorize it [the relationship]. They see us as young actors trying to do that Hollywood-type thing. I hate labels. Johnny's my friend. We are in love. We're 'engaged' . . . but it's deeper than that. He's part of me, important to me right now."

After a few years, they sold their homes and divided their time between an apartment in San Francisco—which became Winona's favorite city ("What other one would name a street after Jack Kerouac?")— a loft in New York City, and a new home in the Hollywood Hills. Eventually, they gave up the apartment in the Big Apple. "It didn't work out in New York," Winona grumbled, "I couldn't deal with the fact that if I got hungry at night I couldn't go anywhere because of the crime factor. Why live that way by choice? And I was too far away from my parents."

Call it homesick or lovesick or sick of love, Winona was still swigging cough syrup and lighting Camel cigarettes when *Select* magazine interviewed her for their July 1991 issue in an article called "Meet the Happy Couple." She sat in their Manhattan loft just before they moved out. She was nineteen and confident, but suffering with another bout of her recurring respiratory infection and silently suffering the end of her relationship with Depp. For now, she had to keep up a good front, but she was no longer having a good time. She tried to work it out with him.

Johnny and Winona had a lot in common. He loved to talk to her about books, and Jack Kerouac, and Winona's father loved him. That, more than anything, urged Winona to keep trying. Her father once pulled Winona aside and said, "Marry him!" Her parents would bring them breakfast in bed when they visited.

It was the publicity of the romance that finally brought them down. "I keep hearing that I'm having an affair with so-and-so, I'm pregnant, I'm a drug addict—they've said everything under the sun," she said.

In November 1992, in one last desperate attempt, she reached for the stars to save their blinking love affair. She bought Johnny a star in the Star Registry for forty-five dollars and for another forty-four dollars more she got him a framed certificate showing where the star is located. It's in the Northern sky in the constellation Cepheus and it's called "Jun," which Winona chose as a variation of Johnny.

She abandoned all plans for college during this time, and she seemed very sad about the decision. "I may have to leave because I get an offer of something I am dying to do," Winona sighed. "That's not fair to the school and it would just screw me up. And I don't want to knock college, but I went to visit a friend at a college, and I got there and it was like a frat hell or sorority hell or whatever it is called."

The romance was fast, furious, intense, unstable, and, in her own words, "embar-

When her passionate romance with Depp ended, Winona dressed in black and found solace in working with director Jim Jarmusch, and played a small part in his highly regarded arthouse hit, *Night on Earth*. PHOTO BY ADAM SCULL, GLOBE PHOTOS, INC., © 1992.

rassingly dramatic." Things were seriously wrong but, "I was acting like everything was okay. Smiling. I was being watched all the time." Her illnesses got worse and a doctor diagnosed "anticipatory anxiety" and "anticipatory nostalgia."

She took sleeping pills and feared getting hooked, but her future costar and friend Michelle Pfeiffer helped her kick the habit. "She told me to flush them down the toilet," Winona said. She did.

Her parents visited her in Portugal while she was on set there for *The House of*

the Spirits, but she didn't see them much. She stayed in her hotel room, played the sad Tom Waits's album *Nighthawks at the Diner*, concocted screwdrivers from the minibar and smoked lots of cigarettes—a habit Johnny left her with. He once said he loved smoking so much if he had two mouths he'd smoke out of each of them.

One night she fell asleep with a lit cigarette but woke up before anything caught fire. That incident shook her up big time. She hadn't quite hit rock bottom, but that was as far as she wanted to go.

After the Depp debacle, Winona finally found both a friend and a lover in Soul Asylum's Dave Pirner. PHOTO BY GREG VIE, GLOBE PHOTOS, INC., © 1994.

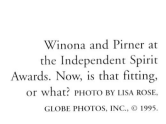

Winona and Pirner at the Independent Spirit Awards. Now, is that fitting, or what? PHOTO BY LISA ROSE, GLOBE PHOTOS, INC., © 1995.

One of the things that saved her during this time was a small role in a small movie *Night on Earth*, directed by independent director Jim Jarmusch. It was an easy role and a small part as a taxi driver named Corky. She drove past many of her old houses in the film—in fact she passed the neighborhood where she lived with Heather. She was driving Gena Rowlands, playing a casting agent, and Gena tried to get the cabbie into the movies.

Corky drives the casting agent to Beverly Hills, up Beverly Drive, past Beverly Boulevard, and onto Beverly Court. It's an inside Los Angeleno joke because everything in Beverly Hills tries to capitalize on the Beverly name. Corky also trashes men a great deal, saying they're not good for anything.

It's a small role, but it gets noticed, and it pulled Winona out of the dumps. Friends such as Matt Dillon, Sean Penn, and Ethan Hawke came to the premiere to see Winona. Johnny didn't show.

Corky finally says to the casting agent in the film, "Look lady, I know the movies and all, I see you're being serious, but that's not real life for me." Per-

haps, that's when Winona decided a public relationship wasn't real life either.

Then came the public announcement that Winona was calling off her engagement to Johnny on June 21, 1993. "They're young and grew apart," the statement said very simply.

"When you fight with your boyfriend, you start acting—it's like work. I've worked with every young actor. Usually they have a problem, or they're fucked up, or they're recovering," Winona said. "Dating an actor is seeing each other on billboards. And breaking up was like *The Neverending Story* because it was such a public thing. We didn't know how to break up."

Winona attended the Columbia Pictures' *Boyz N the Hood* premiere on June 27, 1991 alone, surprisingly, less than a week after the break-up announcement. She talked to reporter Michael Szymanski from *US* magazine while at the red carpet reception for the stars and at the fundraiser at the Twenty/20 Club in Century City. She said she was feeling fine, but wasn't too convincing.

Night on Earth

YEAR:
1991

STARRING:
Gena Rowlands, Winona Ryder, and Roberto Benigni

BILLING:
First (according to appearance)

DIRECTOR:
Jim Jarmusch

RATING: *PG-13*

RUNNING TIME:
98 minutes

WINONA'S CHARACTER'S NAME:
Corky

At the *Boyz* party, she seemed a bit more animated, and chatted to cast members Ice Cube, Cuba Gooding, Jr., Morris Chestnut, Laurence Fishburne, writer/director John Singleton, and others in attendance.

Winona didn't often attend premieres, but was on the list for the *La Femme Nikita* party the next month. She really wanted to see the film, but she was a no-show there, her publicist said, because she was ill again.

While diminutive Winona walked past the camera crews at *Boyz N the Hood*, they yelled "Madonna! Madonna!" because of her straight black hair and because of the bodyguards who surrounded her. She smiled and said, "No, *Winona*" and kept going.

"Where's Johnny?" she was then asked.

She stopped momentarily, looked almost nostalgic, then looked right at the cameras and shrugged.

Winona plays Corky, a Los Angeles cab driver, who gives Victoria (Gena Rowlands in the back seat) a memorable ride. PHOTO COURTESY OF PHOTOFEST.

CHAPTER 10

Brave Winona's Dracula

"It didn't work at all, it was very upsetting. He's very, er, experimental, I guess, and I certainly didn't appreciate it. I just get pissed off when somebody screams at me. I don't cry, I just glare."

—WINONA ABOUT GARY "DRACULA" OLDMAN, SCREAMING AT HER

Looking pensive in her role as Mina. Even though it was at her urging that Francis Ford Coppola made the movie, she did not enjoy the experience. PHOTO COURTESY OF MOVIE STAR NEWS.

Would he be mad at her? Winona had to take the chance. In retrospect, Winona discounted her ultimate responsibility for Francis Ford Coppola making *Bram Stoker's Dracula*, but it truly was her idea from the outset.

"I didn't actually set the film up, all I did was find the script," Winona said. "Actually, the movie didn't turn out to be anything like the script I read; there were no effects in that one, it was like this whole intellectual journal. I gave it to him, met with him, and he said he'd do it."

After changing talent agencies, she was flooded with scripts. She came across a Dracula story by James V. Hart. It was written more as a woman's sexual awakening than as a horror story. A budding fan of British television, she at first agreed to do the movie as a television movie with British director Michael Apted, then she had a chance to talk again to Francis.

They hadn't spoken for half a year. He was still a bit wounded after she turned down *The Godfather III*, and she was worried for a long time that he would sue her for breach of contract.

Winona saw the vampire story as a feature film. Coppola called to meet with her. Winona was startled. "I was like, 'He would?' I mean, I always knew that there was no weirdness between me and him. But I was surprised he wanted to possibly work with me again, because of all the controversy."

Winona met him near San Francisco, up the winding trail of his ranch in Napa Valley. "She said, 'Oh, I have this script I love,'" the director recalled. That seemed to be enough. As much as she insisted she didn't have anything to do with behind the scenes work, she certainly had an eye for talent, suggesting Keanu Reeves for the part of her fiance and agreeing to play the part of Mina.

Coppola had won Best Picture Oscars with the first two parts of his *Godfather* tril-

Bram Stoker's Dracula

YEAR: *1992*

STARRING:
Gary Oldman, Winona Ryder, Anthony Hopkins, and Keanu Reeves

WINONA'S BILLING:
Second

WRITTEN BY:
James V. Hart (based on the novel by Bram Stoker)

DIRECTED BY:
Francis Ford Coppola

RATING: *R*

RUNNING TIME:
122 minutes

WINONA'S CHARACTER'S NAME:
Mina Murray/ Elisabeta

ogy, but he stumbled with the last episode and needed a comeback, and needed to show he could do it under budget. For that, he needed actors he could depend on. He landed Anthony Hopkins and went out on a limb with newcomer Sadie Frost as Lucy, foregoing the more experienced Ione Skye and Juliette Lewis. He gathered Cary Elwes, Richard E. Grant, and Bill Campbell as Lucy's suitors, and singer Tom Waits as the madman Renfield.

A casting call for the lead role went out, and Daniel Day-Lewis would have been perfect, but he was already committed to *The Last of the Mohicans*. Andy Garcia balked about the explicit sex scenes; others inquired and visited Coppola's ranch, such as Armand Assante, Gabriel Byrne, Viggo Mortensen, Antonio Banderas, and Gary Oldman. Gary was the most far-out choice and he wasn't as handsome as Coppola originally envisioned, yet he got the part.

Winona couldn't depend on the sarcastic eye-rolling and sighing she'd done in past

One of the principle reasons Winona did not like making *Dracula* was that she detested working with her costar, Gary Oldman. PHOTO COURTESY OF COLUMBIA PICTURES, © 1992.

roles. She came smack face-to-face with The Method for the first time, via acting coach Greta Seacat, who was hired by Coppola. She also clashed with his harsh tough-love style of directing. To get her upset, Coppola spat insults at her. It meant being called, "bitch, whore, and slut" a lot. The acting coach helped Winona challenge those emotions.

"She [Seacat] opened a lot of doors inside me that I didn't know existed," Winona reflected reluctantly. "I suppose you should do that all the time."

Winona said she always instinctively knew the method of conjuring up emotions from inside, but now everything was important, from a reaction shot of one word to walking down the street, off-camera, always completely in character.

Nothing was more evidence of that fact than star Gary Oldman, who seemed to be in character twenty-four hours a day. Winona didn't much like Oldman, and when she talked about him she would start feeling ill. It got to the point she couldn't stand to be in the same room with him. The feeling seemed mutual.

"I read I was having an affair with Winona Ryder," Oldman taunted cruelly. "Well of course it makes sense doesn't it? The truth of the matter is I slept with Johnny Depp and Winona found out." He smiled.

Winona, however, got in her own licks.

The vampire wedding scene to her was a very romantic, passionate scene where Mina is seeing the man who killed her best friend. She couldn't allow her character to just ignore that and say, "Oh, I love you." The director told her to get mad at him.

"You mean, I have permission to do whatever?" she asked.

So, she jumped on Oldman's back and hit him screaming, "You murderer, you killed my best friend and you say you love me!" and she really got into it. It was the first and only time she would shock her costar. She said, "He was just very emotionally on edge. It wasn't like we hated each other. It's just that we both did our own thing."

She was amazed how he could turn on tears at a snap of the fingers, and she recoiled as she remembered how he would make obscene gestures at her to irritate her.

"When you're doing a love story, you don't always know how close you should get to the person, especially if you don't know them really well," Winona said. "And you always are scared that you're going to get taken advantage of. It's a weird trusting that happens. It's really hard to do unless you really know the person. I'm not saying that Gary and I had a bad working relationship, we just . . . it was. . . . It was odd."

The love scenes were always particularly hard for Winona; she said it was because she didn't know him. "He's English and he's from a different world than I am. He's thirteen years older than me, and I still don't feel like I ever met Gary Oldman, but I feel like I met everyone else."

Dubbing him "The King of Pain," Winona saw Oldman force himself to not eat, sleep less, and find that sense of loss he shows in the film. "It's like if someone's depressed. When you play these characters, they get into your bones," she said.

Oldman said, "We [he and Winona] got on okay. We had very difficult scenes to do and it comes with a certain amount of tension and friction."

The director said, "The issue was not only that they did not get along. They got along and then one day they absolutely didn't get along. I don't know what happened."

Oldman kidded slyly and proudly, "I think I kind of injected a bit of hate."

Meanwhile, off the set Oldman had his own battles. He was picked up and charged with drunk driving after a night on the town with Kiefer Sutherland, earning him a six month driving ban and eighty-nine hours of house arrest. He had just finished his portrayal as Lee Harvey Oswald in *JFK*.

Particularly edgy and unnerved, Winona was even accosted by the normally nice Hopkins in one of the final scenes where Mina is found with Dracula. Before the scene, he started a raucous refrain off

Winona on Dracula

"Dracula *was like a ride. It was wild and chaotic and everyone was running around and chasing each other with fangs.*"

camera of calling her "whore" and "slut."

When Mina awakened from a trance the same thing happened: her acting coach cried out "unclean unclean!" from off stage. Then, Coppola watched her hiding her head so she wouldn't laugh, and started yelling, "You WHORE! You fucking WHORE! You! Look at you! Look at yourself!"

The sudden attacks often made her sob, but then the director wanted eight takes so the "torture" was prolonged. Coppola kept pouring fake blood on her. *Premiere* magazine was there and wrote about every bloody drop.

Winona hated the technique. "Oh, yeah, it was really great. I love being called a bitch and a whore," she said sarcastically. "It's a completely silly technique, and it does not work. I would never have bad-mouthed *Dracula*, but luckily, I don't need to be Francis Coppola's favorite actress to have a good career."

The strain with Coppola grew so intense that much of the time he would talk to the acting coach, who would relate to Winona what was required, rather than talking directly to the actress.

Coppola said, "It does get raw, but I'm trying to capture something that is happening rather than something that's pre-planned. It gets pretty crazy, but they like it."

Even Keanu uncharacteristically got into the name-calling. Winona was surprised: "I had to have this breakdown. All of a sudden I heard Keanu's voice calling me names, like, 'Whore, how could you do this?' I just really started to cry all of a sudden and I did it about fifteen times without a cut. I love Keanu, I really loved working with him and I loved his character. But Gary—"

Was it fun? That became a hard question to answer. "I had fun because the cast and a lot of the crew were very fun people. I mean fun is such a fucked up word anyway, what is fun? You can really have a fun time without being happy, but it was fun."

Some things definitely were not fun. Winona's fear of fire caused real shouts of terror in a scene where flames were sweeping in with Hopkins.

"I was crying," Winona remembered. "At one point his leg caught on fire and I was putting it out. But Anthony was very protective every time, and at the cut he would lift me up and hold me."

For a long time after, Hopkins would see her and remind her, "Remember the rat?"

Yes, rats also were used, lots of them, but Coppola said they never touched the actors. "More exaggeration," waved the director, "they were a mile away."

This would be one of the most sensual *Dracula*s ever made. James V. Hart's script was inspired by primal passions he placed on the real-life historical figure of Vlad the Impaler, a knight who helped save Walachia and Christianity from the Turks in 1476. He was very much in love with his new bride.

In the movie, Winona is shown in the first scene as Vlad's bride throwing herself into the river when word comes back that he is killed in battle. The film opens from

Winona much preferred working with Keanu Reeves. She developed a warm, respectful personal relationship with the often maligned actor. The nature of that relationship is mirrored in the admiring gazes they are exchanging. PHOTO COURTESY OF COLUMBIA PICTURES, © 1992.

there; there are no credits at the beginning. In the next scene, Prince Vlad renounces God and impales much of the innocent townsfolk in his kingdom. He searches for the reincarnation of his lost love. The story jumps to London four centuries later. There, an unknowingly reincarnated Winona is betrothed to Keanu Reeves.

"We can be married when I return," says a stiff Keanu. Not married yet, Winona and Keanu kiss a big kiss in a fanciful garden that has peacocks running around it.

Once again, Winona's character keeps a diary. With her best friend Lucy, she looks through *The Kama Sutra*. Mina says, "Ooh they're disgustingly awful. I don't understand it. Can a man and a woman really do that?"

Mina confesses that she and her suitor have only kissed, "That's all." Lucy laments her lack of lustful experience: she is almost twenty and "practically a hag."

Things soon start to get weird. Mina and Lucy share a kiss in the garden labyrinth and Keanu finds himself in a castle with a two-headed woman's heads between his legs.

In town, Mina comes across the cocky count played by Oldman and tells him curtly, "If you seek culture, then go to a museum. London is full of them."

Later, Dracula and Mina drink absinthe together and get bombed while Keanu is in an orgy.

Sir Hopkins had a great time playing Doctor Van Helsing who helps destroy Dracula, and when he dances with Mina he takes particular joy from the scene. Then, in front of Mina, he asks her betrothed, a befuddled Reeves, "Did you taste the blood of the demonic women?" and Keanu answers, "I was impotent with fear."

After her first bite (it takes three to become a full-fledged vampire), Mina gets fangs and asks Van Helsing, "Will you drive a stake through my heart and cut my head off like [her friend-turned-vampire] Lucy?"

It gets campy and bloody. No one knew how it would play to audiences.

In San Diego, a preview audience was repulsed and confused after seeing a rough cut of the film, but the director had thirty-seven different versions of the film, and opted for the more romantic version. "I did use the metaphor of blood as a symbol of life's passion," admitted Coppola. "And maybe too much, but it's interwoven with themes of love."

Although it didn't win the accolades most hoped it would, the film did win the Academy Award for Best Costume Design and was nominated for Best Production Design.

Oldman, not considered sexy enough and too bizarre for the role by many critics, couldn't carry the picture. In the final take of his final scene, Coppola asked the actor to play it loving and erotic as Coppola read Winona's lines.

"Give me peace," Oldman cried. The spotlight dimmed on his creeping eyes, and he died again.

CHAPTER 11

The Loss of Innocence

"She [represented] all that was best in this world, all that he honored and she anchored him to it."

—WINONA'S MAY TO DANIEL DAY-LEWIS'S CHARACTER, NEWLAND, IN *THE AGE OF INNOCENCE*

*P*rophetically, she said it herself. Winona didn't need Francis Ford Coppola to "make it" in the business. She needed Martin Scorsese.

It was, after all, her role in *The Age of Innocence* (1993) which finally put her in the big league. Now, she was fully legal, a twenty-one-year-old with responsibility, and the competition was growing fierce.

She befriended the screenwriter Jay Cocks, who wrote the adaptation of *The Age of Innocence* from the Edith Wharton book. "Winona is always taking the right steps, even if she's wearing Doc Martens," he concluded, nicknaming her "Radio Free Winona," because she always speaks her mind about anything, and quite freely.

She wasn't a surefire pick for the character of May, said producer Barbara DeFina. "It took a long time to cast her part. We needed someone who was a good physical contrast to Michelle [Pfeiffer] but also someone who could

This classy poster captures the passion and poetry of Martin Scorsese's elegant movie. PHOTO COURTESY OF PHOTOFEST.

carry out the dual nature of May [Welland, the character's name]. There's a complete girlishness in her."

It impressed Scorsese that Winona not only read the book, she read a great deal of Wharton's novels and was totally familiar with their mood.

Shooting began on March 26, 1992 outside Troy, New York and finished at the end of June in the Paris Academy of Music in Philadelphia at Louvre River Street downtown. The small picturesque town of Troy was transformed into the Wall Street of the 1870s. Extensive decorating took place, especially the transformation of a men's fraternity house into a dowager's salon.

The set of *Age* was the first time Winona became awestruck over the cos-

tumes and decor. "It's like watching a movie in itself!" she told one journalist.

She found out quickly she hated the awkward, gaudy outfits. She thought *Bram Stoker's Dracula* was bad as far as costume fittings were concerned. Here she spent a full two hours getting into large beautiful outfits, with her hair always pinned up, and a corset restricting her already tiny frame. She found the costumes stifling to act in, too.

She enjoyed working closely with Scorsese, however, and called him Marty, along with a very select few other performers (a privilege reserved for the likes of Sharon Stone, Al Pacino, Robert DeNiro, and Francis Ford Coppola). Instead of having her pour more emotions on like her

Winona shows off her engagement ring. She also shows off her figure in the film's extraordinary costumes. PHOTO COURTESY OF PHOTOFEST.

previously demanding director, Scorsese had her cut back—way back.

"My performance was very minimalist and Marty kept saying 'less.' I thought I was a Stepford wife." she said. "I've learned more than I have ever learned and it's not just that he talks fast, he's incredibly soothing. He made me feel not only that I was proud of my work, he made me feel great. I actually looked forward to showing up at six in the morning for costume."

Said Scorsese: "I think she's reacting to being part of a labor of love. We had a very good time. Winona has a good sense of humor, and her energy is boundless. It was like having rampant youth on the set. She'd be jumping up and down, but then when you said, 'Action,' she froze into position. All that energy was put behind her eyes, and I found that really fascinating."

During this time, few outside distractions occurred. Most significantly, perhaps, was a little-publicized event when Martin

---

The Age of Innocence

YEAR:
1993

STARRING:
Daniel Day-Lewis, Michelle Pfeiffer, and Winona Ryder

BILLING:
Third

WRITTEN BY:
Jay Cocks and Martin Scorsese (based on the novel by Edith Wharton)

DIRECTED BY:
Martin Scorsese

RATING: *PG*

RUNNING TIME:
133 minutes

WINONA'S CHARACTER'S NAME:
May Welland

Scorsese was picked up by police in Los Angeles one evening while driving through the hills. He was mistaken for a suspect matching the description of the Hillside Strangler, who was responsible for a rash of recent brutal sex crime murders. He was set free, of course.

The film was supposed to be released in the fall of 1992, but was held back almost a year to allow Scorsese more time to edit. And, if you watch closely, the director makes one of his frequent cameo appearances; Scorsese portrays the photographer who takes May's wedding picture.

The story centers on high society of 1870s New York, and Day-Lewis as Newland Archer is unhappily betrothed to the quick but empty-headed May Welland (Winona). Archer reacquaints himself with May's cousin, the scandalous Countess Ellen Olenska, played by Pfeiffer, and he is bound by the etiquette of the time not to act on his feelings.

An "Innocent" Q&A With Winona Ryder

Q: Why choose to play May in *The Age of Innocence*?

W: Aside from the fact that I'd be working with the greatest director ever, and probably the greatest group of people, I was really intrigued by playing a character who was so complex; who you really think is one way and then turns out to be a big surprise at the end. Also, I'm a big Edith Wharton fan, so to be able to try and flesh out one of her characters is kind of an honor.

Q: Did you like May as a person?

W: Yeah. I did like her. I felt a lot of compassion for her predicament. I don't see her as the villain at all. A lot of people feel a lot of different ways; she's one of those characters that people argue about for a long time.

Q: Isn't she manipulative?

W: Well, I think she does what it takes to keep her place in society. I actually think she's much more noble than people give her credit for because she gives him an out a couple of times. I wouldn't say she's manipulative, I'd say she's cunning.

Q: What is her motivation? Is it just to maintain her place in society?

W: Well, yeah, she was raised to be a woman of society, kind of the perfect woman, and the perfect wife, and that's what you do. She wants to keep her place and her family and she doesn't want to disgrace anybody. Things take a turn, and she gives him an option to either stay with what he's promised or back out. I know it may sound weird, but I thought of May as a kind of innocent even though she did those things, but she really kind of started out very innocent.

Q: What was the most difficult thing about achieving her dialect, her style of speaking?

W: You have to rid yourself of all contemporary inflections in your voice. What is it called? You know, ums and uhs. Especially me, I'm like—uhhhh. But I had just done *Dracula*, which was very British and very proper, and I've done theater that takes place back them, so I was a little familiar with it. It was still difficult, because in the etiquette classes I was ridding myself of all contemporary gestures and mannerisms, and things like that. You couldn't scratch your nose or tug your ear or any of that stuff. What if you had an itch? What are you gonna do? I don't know how they made it through the day back then.

Q: What was etiquette class like?

W: It was really scary, you know? You have to even learn when to look up because if you look up at the wrong time, it can be interpreted as flirtation or something. It was very strict. It was a lot of work. I think we should all get a lot more credit than I think people are going to give us, because I worked really hard, and it was difficult. It was like playing tea with your friends when you were little. It was like that but just more strict.

"The subject [matter of the film] was so depressing that I tried to cheer everybody up by singing show tunes."

—WINONA ON THE SET OF *THE AGE OF INNOCENCE*

Q: How did the clothes affect your performance?

W: They really helped me. They were very uncomfortable, but that's how women felt back then and the restrictiveness you feel in the corsets and stuff keep you from making those contemporary gestures. So, it probably bailed me out of a lot of situations where I probably would have messed up.

My corset was seventeen inches. It was really really small. I did feel faint, and then I understood why women fainted so much, cause if they had an emotion and your breathing got at all irregular you'd just go out, just fall down.

Q: What about archery training?

W: I went to this place in New Jersey that was like a range. That was really great because everyone thought I was going to suck and like hit the cameraman with my arrow, but I got really good at it. I went on the set that day and everyone was really worried about how bad I was going to be and I did it. I like got a bullseye, and everyone was like really impressed!

Q: Would you have liked to live in the 1870s?

W: No, I wouldn't have been because of the clothing and probably for other reasons, but I love period pieces and I'm very fascinated with that time.

Q: What about the sadness of this film. This is such a sad movie . . .

W: Yeah. I remember the first time I read the book, I cried. I was fifteen and it really broke my heart. I was so used to there being good guys and bad guys in books, and here I felt compassion for everyone. I didn't know whose side to be on. The idea of that kind of sacrifice, that like slayed me. I've seen it three times now and I've cried every time. And I never cry in movies that I'm in.

As a result of Winona's stellar performance, honors fell onto the young actress' silk-robed lap. The National Board of Review voted her the Best Supporting Actress and the role earned her a Golden Globe for Best Supporting Actress in a Drama. The film also earned Golden Globe nominations for Best Drama; Best Director for Scorsese; and Best Actress for Pfeiffer.

The film also received many Academy Award nominations: Best Supporting Actress for Winona; Best Original Score for Elmer Bernstein; Best Screenplay Adapted from Material Previously Published in Another Form for Cocks and Scorsese; and Best Production Design by Dante Ferretti. However, only one person took an Oscar home for *The Age of Innocence*, and that was Gabriella Pescucci for Best Costume Design.

Although the film won only one Oscar, it was an honor for Winona just to be nominated by the Academy among such substantial peers as Holly Hunter for *The Firm*, Rosie Perez for *Fearless*, and Emma Thompson for *In the Name of the Father*. Just as in years past in the Best Supporting Actress category, people the world over were scratching their head when the winner was announced as young Anna Paquin for *The Piano*.

When she picked up her Golden Globe two months before the big Academy Awards ceremony, Winona was gracious. "I want to thank Marty, my director," she gushed. "He's just the greatest, he's just the best director in the world. With me, at least, it seems he's telepathic almost."

At her Hollywood Hills home in the psychic haven of Coldwater Canyon, her parents threw her a big party for her Golden Globe win. Godfather Tim Leary was there as was her whole family and a select group of celebrity pals and former costars.

"It was really cool because they've

> *"When the class arranged for a male model to pose nude, I can't tell you how many shades of red Winona turned. As soon as the model walks out in his robe and takes it off, Winona turns scarlet and starts giggling uncontrollably for twenty minutes. She had to move around to the back of the class."*
>
> —MICHELLE PFEIFFER, WINONA'S COSTAR IN *THE AGE OF INNOCENCE*, RECALLS HOW SHE CONVINCED RYDER AND CHER TO TAKE A SCULPTING CLASS

always been so antiestablishment and then I won this award that's aired on TV and everything. They were so excited about it," she said.

She told a magazine that now it was all right for her to finally be a "fucking movie star." She said, "I felt proud as an actress for the first time."

Winona is luminous in *The Age of Innocence*. She might have had a supporting role but it was Winona that everyone was talking about. PHOTO BY PHILLIP CARUSO, COLUMBIA PICTURES, © 1993.

CHAPTER 12

When Reality Really Bites Her

"There was so much drama in my life, I didn't have time for the little things that make life fun and make me happy. I had to get back to a real life."

—WINONA ABOUT THE PERIOD MAKING *THE HOUSE OF THE SPIRITS* AND *REALITY BITES*

Reality bit Winona hard in 1993. She told *Vogue*'s David Handelman that it was a miserable time for her. Just when she thought she was out of her Depp Depression, the world collapsed in on her again. She faced death for the first time closeup when a few of her longtime childhood friends that she had kept in touch with were killed in a freak car accident. Then her first contact with AIDS came when a boy she had been madly in love with as a kid was diagnosed with it, leading to her fundraising for the disease. It became a cause she would champion to this day.

She had to see and hear about her ex-beau Johnny Depp dating supermodel Kate Moss. The new couple were followed everywhere by photographers and Winona couldn't help but hear about them. She wanted to remain friends with Depp but Winona couldn't get in touch with him when he was having personal troubles and went through

Surprisingly Winona had never starred in a bonafide Generation X movie until *Reality Bites*. PHOTO BY VAN REDIN, UNIVERSAL CITY STUDIOS, INC., © 1994.

some nasty arrests. Depp started earning a reputation for trashing hotel rooms as he was dealing with some of his own demons.

And around the same time, New York court records show she was sued by John and Anne Janus for $93,600 for backing out of her lease on an Upper East Side duplex apartment that called for her to pay $3,900 a month for two years. She gave them a check for one month's rent and one month security deposit, but changed her mind about living in Manhattan again and stopped payment. They sued, and it was settled out of court.

All this while she was crunching time again by starting her third big-budget, high-drama, all-out period piece in a row, *The House of the Spirits*, which ended up not being one of her smartest film choices. She was not alone.

The twenty-five million dollar film originally cast director Billy August's wife, Pernilla, in Winona's role,

The House of the Spirits

YEAR:
1993

STARRING:
Meryl Streep, Glenn Close, Jeremy Irons, Winona Ryder, and Antonio Banderas

WRITTEN BY:
Billie August (based on the novel by Isabel Allende)

DIRECTED BY:
Billie August

BILLING:
Fifth

RATING: *R*

RUNNING TIME:
137 minutes

WINONA'S CHARACTER'S NAME:
Blanca Truebas

but the actress got pregnant and couldn't play the part. Winona obliged. "I couldn't believe they chose me. I was really flattered. I felt out of my league. It's hard to forget that you're working with Meryl Streep."

Winona couldn't pass up this project. She was asked to play Blanca Truebas, a woman who was abused by her father, lost her mother, raised a child out of wedlock, and was tortured in prison. The cast list included the greats: Streep, Jeremy Irons, Glenn Close, new-star-on-the-rise Antonio Banderas, with whom Winona would share a love scene.

She soon found she couldn't sleep again. Filming was just on the tail end of her final breaking of her ties with Depp—cutting off all ties proved too hard at first. Winona said, "It was one of those things where I was so worried about getting sleep that I couldn't fall asleep. I had this digital clock, and every time I barely opened my eyes, I saw these huge red numbers saying 3:30 A.M. and I'm thinking, OK, I have two and a half hours before I have to get up."

The project, also known as *Das Geisterhaus*, was based on the novel by Isabelle Allende and followed three generations of the Truebas family, a wealthy Chilean clan, who are embroiled in social, economic, and political upheaval.

Winona plays daughter to a Chilean patron (played by Jeremy Irons). She falls in love with a revolutionary played by Banderas and both Winona and Antonio are imprisoned and tortured after the 1973 military coup.

Time magazine's April 1994 review by Richard Schickel trashed the film, comparing Glenn Close to Cloris Leachman's outrageous character in Mel Brooks's *Young Frankenstein* (1974), and teases Streep and Irons for their odd aging process and weirdly developing accents. The only one who remains unscathed is Winona; "the simple clarity of her playing redeems the cliche."

"I'm playing this girl who's so lost, and I've never felt so found before," Winona reflected. "This was a time when I ignored myself, I put my career in front of my life. I remember so many of my favorite actors saying 'My work is my life.' And it's not."

The movie starts shockingly enough with Irons off raping a peasant girl, then Irons' character is outraged when finding daughter Blanca skinny-dipping with Pedro, his foreman's son. Fascists stage a coup and the rest, is well, torturous.

Winona joined an all-star cast in the otherwise spiritless *The House of the Spirits*. PHOTO COURTESY OF PHOTOFEST.

You're looking at one of the best moments in the film, the love scene between Winona and Antonio Banderas. PHOTO COURTESY OF PHOTOFEST.

In the movie, Winona gets beaten to a bloody pulp. Her role is like one of the Amnesty cases she writes letters for, and she doesn't recall how she lived through the torture scenes. Sitting on a Utah ski lodge talking to a reporter, she recalled, "I just don't know if I could do it again. It's very violating, even though you're acting, to be handled that way. Because you have to make yourself receptive, so it turns into, well, it's not pretend anymore. There are a couple of things you can't fake. When someone picks you up by the hair, when you're being dragged through the street—you can't fake that. To a certain degree you have to get hit. The hardest thing is being blindfolded and handcuffed and you don't know where the hit is coming from and you don't know when."

Vincent Gallo, playing her half-brother and tormentor, Esteban, became a close friend of Winona's. After each take, they were hugging. Yet, by the end of the ordeal, she was covered with bruises and welts and her shoulder felt dislocated.

"Life itself has become the most important thing," her voice-over says in the film. For Winona, the words rang truer than any she had heard in a long time.

Getting her life in order following the filming of *Spirits* first meant dealing with some health issues. She went to a sleep clinic in Florida to help her insomnia and discovered, "The insomnia was really a symptom of something else, which worried me at first, but then made perfect sense. I mean, when you spend your most crucial adolescent years being watched by millions of people and being told what's good and what's bad, you have no sense of who you are," Winona said.

Taking a prescription drug to relieve insomnia addicted her for a brief time, but it was all kept quiet and never reported; she certainly didn't have the problems of most of her youthful peers. She didn't know the medication she was taking was quite so addictive and she said, "The doctor literally said, 'You can eat them like candy.' When I realized I needed them, I stopped taking them."

> *"The camera really does love her. It can't seem to get enough of what she holds in her eyes."*
>
> —MERYL STREEP

People congratulated her for performances that were painful for her to do, and even painful for her to remember. People told her she would win awards for roles she hated, and for scenes that were painful memories, that she could not watch again on the big screen.

"I started thinking, 'God, did I? Was it

Meryl Streep and Glenn Close play a mean game of badminton in *Spirits*. They generated about as much drama in their little game as the movie did on the big screen. PHOTO COURTESY OF PHOTOFEST.

good that I was going through all that?' I decided, I don't care if someone says, 'You're going to win every award in the world for this performance, but you could have only done it because you were going through that stuff.' I'd still go back and want to be really happy, and be bad in the movie!" Winona reflected. "You don't have to be miserable to be a good actress." she decided.

Part of her misery was from still getting over Johnny Depp, she knew that. "I was just really young. I don't know what his excuse is, but that's mine!" She turned to music, and then she met David Pirner, the rock singer of Soul Asylum at an *MTV Unplugged* taping in 1993. It was almost love at first sight.

"Music was the one thing that helped me through my depression," Winona said, "I was very surprised when I saw him [Pirner] and he had red hair. The pictures on the CDs are really small."

She was forward, and invited him over to her house in Los Angeles for pizza. They ordered a Dominos with mushrooms. "Our schedules didn't really allow picnics at the beach. But it was still very romantic."

They talked so much the pizza got cold. Winona said, "I wanted to fry it, and he said, 'That's impossible,' because he thought after being in a band for seven years he knew every trick for heating up pizza. But I totally fried it! It was like a montage sequence."

It must have hurt Johnny Depp to hear that Winona began dating Pirner since

Depp originally came to L.A. to be a rock star. Pirner left his girlfriend of eleven years for Winona. The Minneapolis singer with a mane of pseudo dreadlocks was seen smooching with her at the Twin Cities Bowling Alley. They went to New Orleans and walked down the streets doing Jell-O shooters. She was reckless.

Pirner, after all, was really only her second boyfriend—she doesn't include the two weeks with *Heathers*'s costar Christian Slater. To this point, she'd been linked with lots of stars, but insisted, "None of that was true. None of the costars except for Christian, who I went out with for two weeks and he broke my heart. Dave is only like my second boyfriend. Yes, but I'm still innocent. I'm just not so naive. Maybe I'm getting innocent mixed up with corny. I feel I still have a lot to learn, but that doesn't make me innocent, does it?"

To make sure, for a magazine story, she polled her friends—Kevin, Helene, Charlene, Rick, Heather—and asked them, oh-so-casually, "Do you think of me as being innocent?"

They all answered a resounding, "Yes!"

"And pure? I think I'm pretty pure. I don't know. Every day is a struggle to be these things, but it's worth it. It's really easy to be depressed and be a bad person, and dishonest, and it's hard to be good and honest and happy. It takes effort, it's scarier, but it's so much better," she said.

Pirner laid the ground rules from the

beginning: "Everybody I know is second string to music for me." That included Winona.

Her fame sometimes baffled him. Winona said, "He called me and said he'd gone into a truck stop in Oklahoma City to play pinball, and after he started, he realized he was playing the Winona Ryder *Dracula* pinball machine. He said, 'I couldn't tell if it made my day or ruined my game.' "

"I'm twenty-three and I want to act my age. Do things that people my age do. I don't have to suffer to be good," Winona declared. When anyone brought up her rumored four million dollars a picture asking price she replied, "Oh, shut up!"

Tired of period pictures, tired of uncomfortable dresses, she wanted to get back to her peers and agreed to do a satire. Her agent called her up and said, "I think you're going to like this movie, because you can wear jeans in it."

Fine. Was there a role for her boyfriend? Dave Pirner suddenly got bitten by the acting bug, wanted to try a role, and

Reality Bites

YEAR:
1994

STARRING:
*Winona Ryder,
Ethan Hawke,
Ben Stiller,
Swoosie Kurtz, and
Janeane Garofalo*

WINONA BILLING:
Top

WRITTEN BY:
Helen Childress

DIRECTED BY:
Ben Stiller

RATING:
PG-13

RUNNING TIME:
99 minutes

**WINONA'S
CHARACTER'S NAME:**
Lelaina Pierce

since he always seemed to be hanging around the set anyway, why not? She'd get him a role. The film was *Reality Bites*.

Pirner did well in the role of Phineas even though he had never acted before, and he had a great time in his small role. The director and costar of the film, Ben Stiller—not wanting to lose Winona's star power—was only too glad to give Pirner the role at Winona's request. However, Stiller noted that he would never have cast Pirner if he wasn't right for the part.

The script surprised her. She read it in one sitting, which she doesn't usually do. "It was obvious that this was a screenplay written by someone young and of my generation," Winona said. It was a sort of autobiographical story by twenty-three-year-old first-time screenwriter Helen Childress about a girl who graduates as valedictorian from college, gets fired from her first job and then can't even find work at Wendy's.

Reality Bites was something Winona could identify with immensely. "It was very true to life. I understood the character Lelaina and my impression of her was that she said the things I could only wish I would think of on the spot, instead of later in the car on the way home," Winona analyzed.

The unemployable documentary filmmaker has a relationship with a young, unemployable love interest Troy, played by Winona's real-life Manhattan pal Ethan Hawke. Troy threatens to turn her apartment into "a den of slack." She has to chose between him and the stiff executive, played by director Stiller. Lelaina and Troy are afraid to jeopardize their platonic brother-sister friendship by having sex. That's the story.

Winona loved the cast, including Janeane Garofalo, fresh from TV's *The Larry Sanders Show*, and newcomer Steve Zahn and it turned out to be a close-knit cast. They all flew out to Houston for a few weeks to film. She spent as much time with Janeane as she did with her boyfriend David, and they ate lots of junk food in their trailers and hung out.

She became close pals with director Stiller, Zahn (Sammy Gray), Swoosie Kurtz (Charlane McGregor), Harry O'Reilly (Wes McGregor), and Susan Norfleet (Helen Anne Pierce). She loved the actors in some of the smaller roles, and treated them all as equals.

"I didn't make it because it was a smart film to make," Winona said, defending her choice. "I did it because it had something to say to people my age and I don't think Hollywood takes them seriously at all."

What was Winona doing? a lot of bigtime Hollywood studio executives were asking. "A lot of people told me, 'You just did a Scorsese movie! You can't do this young, first-time director project,' " Winona laughed. "And I said, 'Why am I concerned with being older? I have

Winona Says to Figure It Out for Yourself

"I don't want to be the spokesperson of my generation. I don't want to be any sort of leader. People should really find out for themselves how they feel about things. I hate it when actors start talking about something and they get asked a question and they don't know how to answer it. That's so embarrassing. I won't put myself in that position."

Winona and Ben Stiller share a moment. Stiller not only costarred as Ethan Hawke's rival in the movie, he also directed it. PHOTO BY VAN REDIN, UNIVERSAL CITY STUDIOS, INC., © 1994.

plenty of time for that!' Also, a lot of people my age have come up to me and said, 'Why don't you do a movie about us?' For some reason people think it's less serious to do a movie with young people."

Sure, there were references to bands, MTV, clothes from The Gap, and other "Generation X" terms that older people may not understand. Winona found herself at the Sundance Film Festival defending the film.

The reality is, for the most part, she thought the finished movie bit.

"I just saw it last night for the first time," she said at the film festival. "I guess I always knew it was a love story, but while I was doing it my focus was on my character's work—that she has been laboring over this documentary for a long time and does not want to see it commercialized. But the script for *Reality Bites* was very different from how the movie turned out, and most of us were feeling as if what was happening to my character's documentary was also happening to the movie. Still, Universal was a lot more liberal than I expected them to be. I don't think studio heads quite get the joke about The Gap, for instance, but they left it in the movie."

> *"I am not under any orders to make the world a better place."*
>
> —WINONA
> IN *REALITY BITES*

Ethan Hawke and Winona made a very believeable couple. But there was a real romance going on elsewhere in Winona's life . . . PHOTO BY VAN REDIN, UNIVERSAL CITY STUDIOS, INC., © 1994.

She walked around the independent film festival in overalls, a sweater, boots, and no makeup. People were coming up to her quoting lines, like "I'm bursting with fruit flavor."

Her favorite lines were between Stiller (as Michael Grates) and her character, such as:

Lelaina: So, uh, what religion are you?

Michael: I'm kind of a non-practicing Jew.

Lelaina: That's okay. I'm a non-practicing virgin.

Winona hated that *Reality Bites* was being called a "Generation X" film. She also hated that the attention was drawn toward her and away from some of her more able costars. In January 1994, the National Board of Review gave her a Best Supporting Actress award for *Reality Bites*, and that vindicated her decision for a while. She felt that her best work had not yet been seen by the public, and she wanted *Reality Bites* to be a fitting showcase for her. The award made her feel better, but she felt deep down that

> *"She'd sit in her trailer and eat all kinds of junk food and drink Coke and doesn't try to glam up. She's a poster girl of every Trekkie computer nerd and athlete, too. She's so gorgeous that she crosses over."*
>
> —JANEANE GAROFALO ON "REGULAR GIRL" RYDER

her involvement with the project is what made the film fail.

"There's an obligation to commercialize something when you have a movie star in it," Winona said. "It got slicked up into a music video vehicle. Maybe if I hadn't been in it, it might have stayed small, more real. I don't blame anyone except myself."

Winona, Janeane, Ethan, and Steve move in together. We know a lot of people who would have liked to have shared those digs. PHOTO BY VAN REDIN, UNIVERSAL CITY STUDIOS, INC., © 1994.

CHAPTER 13

Little Woman Growing Up

> "I read it four times when I was a child; my parents wrote a book about Alcott; I was meant to play this role."
>
> —WINONA ABOUT HER ROLE IN *LITTLE WOMEN*

From the moment she saw the face of the little girl, from the moment she heard the story, Winona, the little woman, knew that she had to do something for Polly Klaas.

Little did she know at the time that that "something" would turn out to be a film project dedicated to Polly that would also fulfill a lifelong dream of Winona's: getting another film version made of her favorite book.

Winona was transfixed when, flipping through the news channels, she came upon *America's Most Wanted*. There, she saw a photograph of twelve-year-old Polly who was kidnapped from her Petaluma, California home in 1993, and there on television was Winona's hometown, the familiar streets, and even her junior high school stage where Polly (and Winona) began acting.

"I was like, 'This is an outrage, and it's outrageous that more people aren't outraged.' When something happens to

As always, Winona looks great in period clothing. PHOTO BY JOSEPH LEDERER, COLUMBIA PICTURES, © 1994.

a child, the world should stand still," said Winona, and for her at that moment, the world did.

It disturbed her. She went out for a walk, then she called to help from the lobby of the hotel she was staying at and broke down in sobs. Joanne Gardner of the Klaas Foundation received the actress's first phone call.

Winona bawled, "This is my town. This is my junior high. What can I do? Do you need money?"

Gardner said, "We talked for an hour and a half. Winona had an awful lot of experience, because she'd had some horrible experiences of her own—being stalked and all that. She had some psychologists that she knew. She had some FBI people that she knew. I mean, this woman . . . I've always been a fan, and she's a lovely little woman, but I never thought she would do all this."

Winona flew home immediately. She desperately joined the search for Polly, she helped scour the fields and helped answer

(From left) Christian Bale, Winona, Trini Alvarado and Eric Stoltz. PHOTO COURTESY OF PHOTOFEST.

the hot line. She worried that her involvement would seem like an unabashed photo opportunity, but she didn't care.

"It was the first time I wasn't ashamed of promoting my celebrityism, or whatever you call it," Winona said. "I really felt like I could help."

The kidnapping brought up a lot of issues for Winona. She recalled the past New Year's Eve when a drunken woman came up to her and slapped her on the back spouting off her name. It freaked her out so much she fled back home. She had also been stalked, and threatened by a few different people in past years.

One mistaken impression that came about during the media intensity spotlighting the murder was that Winona knew Polly Klaas before she was kidnapped. That's absolutely not true, but was widely reported as such on television and in print. Winona contacted the family, became close to them, and even stayed with

---

Little Women

YEAR: *1994*

STARRING:
*Winona Ryder,
Trini Alvarado,
Claire Danes,
Kirsten Dunst,
Samantha Mathis,
Gabriel Byrne,
Eric Stolz, and
Susan Sarandon*

BILLING:
Top

PRODUCED BY:
*Columbia Pictures
/ Denise DiNovi*

WRITTEN BY:
*Robin Swicord
(based on the novel by
Louisa May Alcott)*

DIRECTED BY:
Gillian Armstrong

RATING: *PG*

RUNNING TIME:
119 minutes

**WINONA'S
CHARACTER'S NAME:**
Jo March

---

them, but it all took place after the abduction occurred.

The actress made a number of emotional appeals for the child's safe return on news broadcasts. She made a video for the foundation, agreed to serve on their board, and even put Polly's photo in one of her boyfriend's music videos. At first, Winona, with the family, hung onto hopes that Polly would be found alive, but then they found her body.

Polly's father, Marc Klaas, thanked the actress for her help. "She single-handedly put the story back on the front pages by offering a $200,000 reward."

While at the Klaas family's house, Winona noticed the book *Little Women* in Polly's room. She had been reading it again. It was her favorite book, too.

"It really hit me hard," said Winona, who to this day serves on the Klaas Foundation's board of directors. "She lived two blocks away from me. She was missing for two months. It was a twenty-four-hour-a-

True sisterhood. PHOTO BY JOSEPH LEDERER, COLUMBIA PICTURES, © 1994.

A heavenly choir. PHOTO BY JOSEPH LEDERER, COLUMBIA PICTURES, © 1994.

Winona fought to get *Little Women* made, an ensemble piece in which she shared the screen with a considerable number of other formidable actresses: clockwise from the left, Winona, Trini Alvarado, Kirsten Dunst, Susan Sarandon and Claire Danes. PHOTO BY JOSEPH LEDERER, COLUMBIA PICTURES, © 1994.

day search everywhere and I've never been involved in anything like that. I felt pleased that I could help, that I had money to help, and that I had the power to keep it in the press, because the press were refusing to write about it unless I did interviews, which was kind of sick."

Universal Pictures, at Winona's request, turned the February 17 Los Angeles premiere of *Reality Bites* into a benefit for the group, which now helps search for other missing children. She wore a lavender ribbon, saying it was Polly's favorite color.

"I wore her button last night because I don't want people to forget," Winona said. "I've gotten really close to her little sister, who's six and who everyone says has Polly's sense of humor. I really feel

> "*I didn't have to mother Winona too much. She's a very smart, very experienced young woman. I really admire the fact that she's taken her life in her hands. It's hard to start out really young in the business. It's much easier to come in at twenty-six or twenty-seven. It's hard to go through that change on film publicly. Hardly anybody survived from when I was twenty and started [in* Joe *(1970)] and she was even younger. So I have great respect for her. I think she did some of her best work to date in that film. I thought she was just transcendant. I love Winona and I really respect her.*"
>
> —SUSAN SARANDON, WHO PLAYED WINONA'S MOTHER IN *LITTLE WOMEN*, HAS A FEW WORDS TO SAY ON THE SUBJECT . . .

as if I know her in a way. It's ironic, because about six months before it happened, I'd been talking to the National Center for Missing and Exploited Children, trying to figure out something I could do, mostly for runaways. And then this happened next door.

"It's weird, but from the time I was really little, I knew what kidnapping was and it was always my worst fear. I remember so well when Kevin Collins was kidnapped, because he lived in our neighborhood in San Francisco and my sister babysat for him once. And you probably remember that little girl Tars Burke. And I remember Steven Stayner so well because we used to live in Mendocino. I've even had some weird run-ins myself . . . I remember once my sister and I were followed by some people. God knows how many attempted kidnappings there are."

She hoped to make a film featuring a memorable character who served as a role model for young girls. "But everybody was scared of making *Little Women*—no one's going to go and see it, it won't make money and blah, blah, blah—I don't think it would have been made at Columbia unless I said yes, or unless Julia Roberts wanted to do it," Winona said.

She read the book for the first time when she was the same age as Polly, twelve. Her parents wrote about Alcott in two books. Winona thought people could socially benefit from the film.

The only drawback, her friend and *Heathers* producer Denise DiNovi said, were getting back into the "dreaded corset" reminiscent of *Dracula* and *The Age of Innocence*. "I think Hollywood is pretty much run by men who are obviously interested in girls but don't have a real understanding of what

Winona and Christian Bale in a movie that never would have been made had she not pushed to get it done. PHOTO COURTESY OF PHOTOFEST.

Friendship turns to heartbreak when Bale does the unthinkable; he turns Winona down.
PHOTO BY JOSEPH LEDERER, COLUMBIA PICTURES,© 1994.

A handsome film, *Little Women* also had a handsome older man for Winona in the person of Gabriel Byrne. PHOTO BY JOSEPH LEDERER, COLUMBIA PICTURES, © 1994.

Finally, Winona's Jo finds love with Byrne. PHOTO BY JOSEPH LEDERER, COLUMBIA PICTURES, © 1994.

we go through, especially at that young age," DiNovi said. "Look at the kind of movies coming out now. If they have anything to do with women it's pretty aesthetic."

The past movies didn't do the story right as far as Winona was concerned. Katharine Hepburn starred in the 1933 version and June Allyson played a plucky Jo March in 1949. This would be the fourth retelling. "Certainly [this latest incarnation of] *Little Women* became a reality because of Winona's participation," admitted Mark Canton, chairman of Columbia/TriStar. He was never sorry they did it.

Winona wanted to be a mom since the time she was five years old, and since a lot of the cast were around the age of twelve, she got her chance. They all took classes together in needlework, knitting, darning, and pen and ink calligraphy. Winona taught them acting games like Take a Bow.

They filmed on Vancouver Island in an old castle and in Boston, and no story could by more classically American. Writer Louisa May Alcott is considered much too sentimental in Europe, but the story is set in New England at the time of the American Civil War and considered historic fiction.

With Trini Alvarado and Kirsten Dunst. PHOTO COURTESY OF PHOTOFEST.

The four March girls, Jo, Amy, Meg, and Beth, are raised in a single-parent home by their mother, Marmee, while Daddy March is away fighting the war. Marmee teaches the girls morality and individual responsibility, which alienates them from the rest of the town who believe that women should know their place. Women should not be so bold and not live on their own. The script adds material from Alcott's own family. The plot had similarities with Winona's childhood—from transcendentalism to vegetarianism, and animal rights—but there's a 126-year difference.

Jo March, played by Winona, is the raucous tomboy who eschews marriage and instead flees to New York to become a writer.

Normally a story that Hollywood would consider too sweet for another remake these days, Winona managed to get *Little Women* made in a way that made the women good role models for today's young people.

They rounded up a cast of great actors: Susan Sarandon as Marmee, Gabriel Byrne as Professor Bhaer, and Eric Stoltz as John Brooke. Kirsten Dunst (who played a much different character opposite Tom Cruise in *Interview with the Vampire*) and the classic

> *"She's such a complicated person, she's a great person. Winona is funny. She does give me advice. We do hang out. She is a personal hero of mine."*
>
> —CLAIRE DANES, RYDER'S *LITTLE WOMEN* COSTAR

Mary Wickes in one of the last roles before her death, joined the very strong cast.

Australian director Gillian Armstrong, responsible for one of Winona's favorite films, *My Brilliant Career* (1979) seemed like a natural pick to direct. The director loved Winona from the outset: "It was delightful to work with someone as fine tuned as she is; it's like having this most perfect musical instrument to play."

Winona's friends got involved. Claire Danes, then the budding star of TV's *My So-Called Life* offered up a stunning performance as the ailing Beth. Winona also suggested Trini Alvarado as Meg and Samantha Mathis as a grown-up Amy. They tested others, but went with Winona's instincts. (She later recommended all three to work in Winona's next film, *How to Make an American Quilt*.)

Winona declared John Turturro (who starred in *Barton Fink*) the sexiest actor working today and she wanted him to play the older professor that Jo meets and falls for. Columbia nixed him in favor of Gabriel Byrne.

The $19 million movie was narrated (as usual) by Winona, and the film made its money back quickly. Filming with a mostly female crew was a good experience; Winona

Activism

Winona's activist roles in her private life and the causes she takes under her wings

➤ Winona writes letters for Amnesty International to this day.

➤ She contributed to the construction of the United States Holocaust Memorial Museum in Washington, D.C.

➤ She is concerned with the sexual abuse of children and wants to make a movie about it.

➤ She offered a $200,000 reward for the kidnapped Polly Klaas's safe return, manned phones, went on a search for her, and befriended her sister, Annie.

➤ Polly Klaas's picture was put on the Soul Asylum rock video and on the album.

➤ Winona used the internet computer alert system to help locate Polly when she was first missing.

➤ She worked in the Nuclear Freeze movement.

➤ She took a part in her mother's AIDS video project in 1987.

➤ She taped a public service announcement for the National Center for Missing and Exploited Children with David Crosby, Paula Abdul, and Angela Bassett.

➤ She is greatly influenced by her very progressive parents.

➤ She pushed to get the movie *Little Women* dedicated to Polly, since it was her favorite book.

At the premiere
of *Little Women* with
rocker boyfriend, Pirner.
PHOTO BY MICHAEL FERGUSON,
GLOBE PHOTOS, INC., © 1994.

With the critical and
commercial success
of *Little Women,* Winona
arrived at the 67th Annual
Academy Awards with both
superstardom *and* Dave
Pirner. PHOTO BY ANDREA RENAULT,
GLOBE PHOTOS, INC., © 1995.

summed, "When you're with a woman, it's different than if you're with a man. You know, sometimes with male directors, and I'm not talking about anyone specific, they are really afraid they are going to offend you. They are really afraid to talk about sexuality and sensuality. They're just scared. You know, 'I'm not coming on to you, but can you do this.' It's just a little more tense when it comes to more sensitive issues."

How did the guys fare in an all-girls' movie? Byrne had them all giggling, and the crew lined up to kiss him after his few days on the set. "Eric Stoltz was great. He's really such a girl's guy. I don't think he felt uncomfortable," Winona said.

Winona did another real-life *Rescue 911* scene involving fire, much like the time she stamped out Anthony Hopkins' pants' legs. Claire Danes told the story to Michael Szymanski from *Entertainment Weekly* in 1996. "On *Little Women* my wig caught on fire. I was walking up the stairs with a candle and she took her own hand and beat it out for me when no one else was even noticing. I was really on fire," said Danes, who recently scored a hit with *Romeo and Juliet* playing Juliet to Leonardo DiCaprio's Romeo. "She's really great at choosing the right roles and I'm not as talented in that area. I'll just go for anything.

"She has actually called me when she's heard that I'm up for something. I'm not as talented in picking and she's called me a few times when she's heard I'm up for some not-

so-great movie and she'll say, 'Claire, Claire, hold on!' in her desperate voice. She's helped me in lots of invaluable ways.

"She is a personal hero of mine," Danes said. "Winona is definitely a major person in my life and my career. *Little Women* was my first major feature and she was very much there for me and was very open to me. I'll always appreciate her for treating me like that."

During this period, Winona had been seen out publicly at music clubs in Hollywood with Dave Pirner. Their relationship apparently had become comfortable. He hung out while she was in the studio, she went on tour with him. At home they'd watch videos like the British TV series *Prime Suspect*. Their relationship is "nice," but Winona means that nicely.

Pirner isn't a tortured artist. He's easygoing, noncombative, and good-humored. She pointed out an ink stain in the middle of the beige carpet to a journalist at her home and said Pirner was writing Christmas cards.

She joked about his hair, saying, "Aww. His hair is fine. He just hasn't brushed it in ten years."

Laying around her house is a photo album from *The Age of Innocence,* in which Scorsese wrote, "To Winona: You 'became' May Welland by incorporating all the delight, beauty, and strength that you already posses." She collects first editions of Jane Austen and E. M. Forster and original letters from Albert Einstein and Oscar Wilde.

Her figure bloomed to the point that after seeing her in a *Vogue* spread, her friends thought that she had breast implants. The idea disgusts her. "I'm way too chicken to go under the knife. The thought of someone touching your breast with something metal is like the most—it's so—I mean, it's horrifying to even think about!"

She started thinking about college again. "I want to educate myself, if I tried to alter myself to what people want to do I would never be challenged. I really want to study English literature, read a lot of classics, take some philosophy classes. I think it will help my work a lot. I read so many scripts, I want to take a break from that. I want to read books and talk about them. I don't want to make a big deal of it. I just want to start by taking some classes. I'm trying to find out how I can do it in a way where I can miss classes and it's not going to fuck me up." It's more important than going to awards shows, she insisted.

And what an awkward year it was when the Academy Award nominations came out. The *Forrest Gump* year ignored *Little Women* for best picture or director, but Winona was up against her friend and *Little Women* "mom," Susan Sarandon, for Best Actress, who was nominated for *The Client. Little Women* was also nominated for Best Original Score (Thomas Newman) and Costume Design (Colleen Atwood).

Winona was given 7:2 odds in Las Vegas for winning Best Actress at the Academy Awards for *Little Women,* and *Entertainment Weekly* predicted: "Fresh without being fey, sincere without being tremulous, Ryder has grown into a performer of unexpected depth and maturity. In *Little Women,* even more than in *The Age of Innocence,* she pulls off the neat trick of creating a credible nineteenth-century heroine for a twentieth-century audience."

For her it was an incredible honor to be up against some of the best actresses ever: Jodie Foster for *Nell,* Jessica Lange for *Blue Sky,* and Miranda Richardson for *Tom & Viv.* Almost everyone knew it was a foregone conclusion that Lange would win—and she did—and everyone also knew that Sarandon and Winona would someday get theirs. Sarandon's time came a year later when she won the Best Actress Oscar for *Dead Man Walking.*

CHAPTER 14

How to Make an American Superstar

"There are no rules you can follow, you have to go by instinct and you have to be brave."

—LINES WRITTEN BY FINN IN *HOW TO MAKE AN AMERICAN QUILT*

Winona liked to read, so it was no wonder she absolutely loved the book *How to Make an American Quilt* by Whitney Otto. Winona believed that the story of such an intricate relationship between women had only rarely been told with such richness.

How ironic that when author Otto heard of Winona's interest, she said, "I couldn't think of anyone better to play the role of Finn than Winona Ryder. I didn't have anyone in mind when I wrote it, but Winona really is Finn."

When her boyfriend proposes marriage, Finn flees to her grandmother, played by Ellen Burstyn, and her aunt, played by Anne Bancroft, and seeks the advice of the sewing circle, who share their stories of love and life. The superb female cast consists of Jean Simmons, Lois Smith, Kate Nelligan, Alfre Woodard, and the poet Maya Angelou. Winona's fellow *Little Women* and friends Samantha Mathis

Winona once again surrounded herself with a cast full of top flight actresses, both young and old. Here she is with, from left, Anne Bancroft, Ellen Burstyn, Alfre Woodard and Kate Nelligan.
PHOTO BY DEBORAH FEINGOLD, UNIVERSAL CITY STUDIOS, INC., © 1995.

and Claire Danes are also cast in the film, but they never share a scene with Winona.

Winona asks the senior women, "How do you merge into this thing called a couple and still keep a little part of yourself?" Winona's character has cheated on Sam, her fiance, played by the handsome Dermot Mulroney; she is seduced by a sexy local.

Before Winona's character has sex with hunk Leon, (Mulroney) there's a line she delivers that Winona may believe strongly herself: "Monogamy is really a very unnatural state that's been forced on us for centuries by screwed up religious leaders who are completely out of touch with their own sexuality."

Jocelyn Moorhouse, director of the dramatic film *Proof* (1992) and screenwriter Jane Anderson, responsible for the riotous HBO movie about the Texas cheer-

How to Make an American Quilt

YEAR: *1995*

STARRING:
Maya Angelou, Anne Bancroft, Ellen Burstyn, Kate Capshaw, Claire Danes, Jared Leto, Samantha Mathis, Dermot Mulroney, Winona Ryder, Jonathon Schaech, Rip Torn, Mykelti Williamson, and Alfre Woodard

BILLING:
Ninth (in alphabetical order)

WRITTEN BY:
Jane Anderson (based on the book by Whitney Otto)

DIRECTED BY:
Jocelyn Moorhouse

PRODUCED BY:
Universal Pictures

RATING: *PG-13*

RUNNING TIME:
109 minutes

WINONA'S CHARACTER'S NAME: *Finn Dodd*

leader's mom, were criticized for the film's similarities to *Fried Green Tomatoes* (1991) and *The Joy Luck Club* (1993). It received mixed reviews.

Richard Schickel of *Time* magazine wrote, "There's something abrupt about the way these ladies are brought forward one by one to tell their often archetypal tales of dreams betrayed. But there's also a nice tartness, a lack of self-pity, in their telling. *Quilt* is a patchwork, but when it's finally stitched together, one sees a certain artless intricacy in its design, a certain glow in its blend of colors." Leah Rozen wrote in *People* magazine, "What can I say, *American Quilt* didn't do it for me, but it obviously got the [tear] ducts in my row. How you react to this episodic tale of female fortitude will depend less on how you feel about quilting than on how susceptible you are to movies in which

By every definition, this was a woman's movie. Unlike *Little Women*, however, women nor men went to see it. Here Winona shares a scene with Maya Angelou and Ellen Burstyn. PHOTO BY SUZANNE TENNER, UNIVERSAL CITY STUDIOS, INC., © 1995.

Winona tries to figure out what to do with her life in *How to Make an American Quilt* and, in this scene, Alfre Woodard tries to help her. PHOTO BY SUZANNE TENNER, UNIVERSAL CITY STUDIOS, INC., © 1995.

Winona's Finn may or may not marry her boyfriend, Sam (Dermot Mulroney). Full of doubts, she heads off to stay with her aunt and gets to know the quilting circle. PHOTO BY SUZANNE TENNER, UNIVERSAL CITY STUDIOS, INC., © 1995.

Each member of her aunt's quilting circle tells Winona a story from the past. Here she's with her aunt, played by Anne Bancroft. PHOTO BY SUZANNE TENNER, UNIVERSAL CITY STUDIOS, INC., © 1995.

In her youth, Jean Simmons (seen here as Em) had something like the same appeal that Winona has today. PHOTO BY SUZANNE TENNER, UNIVERSAL CITY STUDIOS, INC., © 1995.

Winona shares a smoke and a story with Constance (Kate Nelligan). PHOTO BY SUZANNE TENNER, UNIVERSAL CITY STUDIOS, INC., © 1995.

Winona gets to know the local hunk, played by Johnathon Schaech. There is definitely some heat in their scenes together, but the love triangle is only a subplot. PHOTO BY SUZANNE TENNER, UNIVERSAL CITY STUDIOS, INC., © 1995.

women suffer, suffer, and then suffer some more, all for love."

It was during this time that Winona was suddenly noticed as a fashion plate, a term she still scoffs at today. Her short brown hair style from *American Quilt* was photographed and copied by hair salons throughout the country. It was a far cry from the somewhat radical spiked hair she started out with. She experimented with all sorts of different designers, discovering Azzedine Alaia before almost anyone else, but preferred the more casual Comme des Garcons and Barneys.

Hollywood fashion consultant and Las Vegas impersonator Gary Rogers, makeup artist to the stars, analyzed some of Winona's classic looks recently and made some important notations. "In 1989, her eyebrows were very natural and full, there was no stylized shaping," Rogers noted. "In 1990 she is maintaining a youthful look but the eyebrows have been somewhat refined with a definite contour and style unlike the rather wild Brooke Shields look of 1989.

"Look at her in the June 1989 photo spread where she has a pet poodle Peaches on her lap and wears pink ribbons," Rogers said. "She has porcelain skin and wide-set eyes and is decked out in white, with a short brocade dress, a pillbox hat and gloves, looking very Jackie Kennedy. She's seventeen here and a definite rock and roll Lolita."

For Rogers and other fashion experts, one Winona highlight was the 1994 cover of British *Premiere* magazine, which sports a glamorous fashion photo of her looking "as if she just stepped out of a London boutique circa 1966," notes Rogers. "Featuring a thinned out sleek eyebrow, her eyes are quite expressive and doe–eyed and she looks quite Sasoon-like in the pixie cut.

"Winona could pass for Twiggy's younger sibling in that look," Rogers exclaimed. "Five years brought a dramatic change in the way she looks. There's a definite upswing into sophistication and maturing style and the more casual photos in that feature shows she has evolved into a gamin beauty reminiscent of Audrey Hepburn in *Funny Face.*"

This was all after she appeared in *Premiere* magazine, with pixie hair and wearing a corset, when she was named by the magazine as having the Worst Hair that year.

(Elisabeth Shue won the Best Hair honors.) She was also pictured as a princess in a pair of 501s. She earned acknowledgments for her Badgley Mischka outfit at the Oscars, and Giorgio di Sant Angelo put her in a stretch-baby-mesh/Lycra look that set trends throughout the world, after Winona wore it at an awards show.

They called her a "Paris beatnik" and "New York ultra-chic Audrey Hepburn look á la Agnes B." and "*haute couture* Chanel." At the Golden Globe Awards, she first introduced what has now become her signature look: simple, dark, rich, and all in top fashion. It was intended to look 1950s Natalie Wood, and was elegant rather than trashy.

At one point, walking past a Bullock's department store, Winona said, "Stores like this totally scare me. They're so colorful."

She told Paul Attanasio of *Esquire* that her outfits, the glamour-puss lipstick, the coiffure, the pout, the attitude—none of it was hers. It's all borrowed. They belonged to a photographer, a press agent, the fans.

CHAPTER 15

Just One of the Boys

"No one stays innocent forever."

—THE LINE UNDER
WINONA'S PHOTO
IN THE MOVIE POSTER
FOR *BOYS*

Winona thought that if she worked on an independent film, it would get her back to her roots. She loved the fact that her high-powered young movie star friends and former costars—Christian Slater, Keanu Reeves, Rob Lowe—were doing independent films, and this was the time of the discovery of independent superstar director Quentin Tarantino, after all.

Originally entitled *The Girl You Want*, the focus of Winona's next project was immediately taken off her and it was retitled *Boys*. The story focused on a prep-school senior named John, played by Lukas Haas (who is probably best remembered as the little Amish boy, Samuel, in the 1985 film, *Witness*, starring Harrison Ford). John slowly falls in love with a woman named Patty, played by Winona in her first "older woman" role. After he finds her lying unconscious in a field, he hides her in his dorm room.

Looking a little bit like Jane Fonda in *Klute*, Winona plays the older woman for a change. PHOTO BY DEMMIE TODD, © WALT DISNEY COMPANY.

159

The character of Patty is a snobby equestrienne from a local elite family who jumps a fence and hits her head. Haas finds her and drags her back to his dorm. The Disney division of Touchstone greenlighted this improbable story of a jaded Patty rediscovering her innocence through virginal John.

Trouble was brewing right from the beginning. On August 31, 1994, Winona walked off the project because she wasn't happy with the script. She also desperately wanted to star in the remake of *Sabrina* with Harrison Ford, but decided at the last minute she wouldn't tempt fate by trying to outdo her idol Audrey Hepburn.

"I have lots of time," she said at one interview, "because I just dropped out of this movie [*Sabrina*]." She said she initially went bonkers over the *Boys* screenplay and yearned to play this grown-up character. She was not crazy about a subsequent script change which added some sex scenes she deemed totally unnecessary.

The general feeling was that the film had no audience. The story was described by

Boys

YEAR:
1996

STARRING:
*Winona Ryder,
Lukas Haas,
John C. Reilly,
William Sage, and
James LeGros*

BILLING:
Top billing

PRODUCED BY:
Buena Vista

**DIRECTED AND
WRITTEN BY:**
Stacy Cochran

RATING: *PG-13*

RUNNING TIME:
90 minutes

**WINONA'S
CHARACTER'S NAME:**
Patty Vare

many critics as "ludicrous," and she was described as "wildly miscast."

It was kind of like Disney's *Snow White and the Seven Dwarfs*, as Winona felt a kinship to the seven youths on the set. At one point, she was upset by the way her pubescent costars were treated. "When you're fifteen-years-old, or fourteen, or sixteen, and you know if you get a cold you can't stay in bed, that you are costing a production $300,000, and if you get a pimple you're throwing off a whole team of adults who are judging you, well I really suffered, and I didn't have it bad," Winona smiled. "I had it really good, (a) because I had really good skin, and, (b) I had great parents, and (c) I was really successful."

Equestrian training was on the agenda for Winona when transformed into Patty Vare. She practiced on a bucking machine, seen in *Urban Cowboy*. When people heard she was really doing the movie, her friends teased that she was heading from little women to little men.

During *Boys*, she holed herself up in a room and scribbled away at writing her novel, a process she described as "falling into a vortex." She read a biography of Bobby Darin and Sandra Dee, and journalist Peggy Orenstein's study of teen girls while on the set. Her boyfriend David Pirner visited and she sat on his lap. She got terribly bored on the set otherwise, and Pirner smoked constantly with her, teasingly saying, "I'm no quitter."

Her costar Haas attended the Independent Spirit Awards, and told *Entertainment Weekly*'s Michael Szymanski, "I play the lead against Winona, it's a mood story, more than a prescription love story. We fall in love. And it's in the *My New Gun* [1992] style, because it's the same director and after I saw that, now I understand what she is trying to do with it."

He was standing with his mother at the awards and seemed a bit hesitant. "If the producers let her do what she wants with the movie, then it will be great," Haas said, hinting of Disney meddling. He added, "I do a love scene with Winona, but it's toned down, it's fake, and my kissing her is fake, but it's great to do a scene with her."

On the set, Winona befriended twelve-year-old Spencer Vrooman. "What kind of musical instrument would you want to play?" she asked him. "Gee-tar!" he said. So Winona offered him a lesson and he picked it up fast. "You totally have more of a knack

Playing against school boy Lukas Haas in *Boys*. PHOTO BY DEMMIE TODD, © INTERSCOPE COMMUNICATIONS, INC.

What Could Have Been . . .

Movies that Winona turned down or didn't do,
and sometimes that was a good thing.

CHAIN REACTION Keanu Reeves' action-film costar is Rachel Weisz, after the offer was turned down by his friend Winona and Mira Sorvino.

What happened: Oscar-nominated actresses rarely do action flicks—unless an alien is involved.

CHAPLIN Robert Downey Jr. as the star wanted Winona to play Paulette Goddard, but the role went to Diane Lane.

What happened: Scheduling problems kept Winona from doing what would have been a decent cameo.

CLUELESS Casting director Marnie Waxman wanted Winona before Alicia Silverstone was cast.

What happened: "I don't think she [Silverstone] has the range Winona Ryder has," Waxman says. Duh!

COMPANY OF ANGELS A Kathryn Bigelow movie, scheduled to shoot in Spain. Irish pop star Sinead O'Conner, along with Winona, turned down the starring role of Joan of Arc. Winona recommended Claire Danes.

What happened: Heaven can wait.

DESERT BLOOM The first role she was up for, but Winona lost to Annabeth Gish.

What happened: Winona could have had the career of Annabeth Gish. Who?

DON QUIXOTE Winona as the possible love interest for Robin Williams or Sean Connery.

What happened: Seems like an impossible dream.

FROSTY THE SNOWMAN Horror-meister Sam Raimi directs Winona as a little girl trying to cope with the death of her father with the help of the magical snowman.

What happened: Winona grew up.

GODFATHER III Winona dropped from the role after exhaustion, stress, and fever.

What happened: Her replacement, director Francis Ford Coppola's daughter Sofia, is often credited with ruining the picture.

THE HUDSUCKER PROXY One of the few roles Winona Ryder wanted but didn't get. What happened: The role went to Jennifer Jason Leigh and the movie fizzled.

JERRY MAGUIRE The comedy role opposite Tom Cruise went to Renee Zellweger (who starred in flops like Empire Records and The Return of the Texas Chainsaw Massacre) who also beat out Bridget Fonda, Marisa Tomei, and Patricia Arquette. Winona's current asking price of $3 million to $5 million lost her the part.
What happened: Director Cameron Crowe says, "The initial feeling was, to be quite truthful, 'Good—you saved money.' "

MRS. WINTERBOURNE They tried to coax her with costar Shirley MacLaine. "This was a role Marisa Tomei or Winona Ryder could play," says director Richard Benjamin.
What happened: The part went to Ricki Lake and the movie bombed.

OSCAR & LUCINDA Director John Schlesinger's $15 million Australian project costarring Winona and Ralph Fiennes (of Schindler's List [1993]).
What happened: Financing fell through.

OUTLAWS Director John Duigan and producer Denise DiNovi were attached to this female-centered Western.
What happened: Winona won lots of awards and a Western suddenly became undignified.

SABRINA Sydney Pollack desperately wanted Winona to play the Audrey Hepburn role, but Winona said no one could outdo Audrey, even if Harrison Ford is the costar.
What happened: She was right.

SEA OF LOVE Al Pacino and director Harold Becker begged for Winona.
What happened: It was a wash-out.

SHAKESPEARE IN LOVE First Daniel Day-Lewis was playing Shakespeare opposite Julia Roberts, then there was talk of Kenneth Branagh playing the Bard with Winona as his wife.
What happened: The Universal project is stuck somewhere in the universe.

WRESTLING ERNEST HEMINGWAY To costar as a waitress with Robert Duvall and Shirley MacLaine.
What happened: Critical success, but a box office failure.

than most people I know. You were born to rock." The next week, she bought Spencer a guitar.

Boys received some of the worst reviews of any movie of Winona's career. "I feel like I woke up with the dial on the wrong channel or something," John says to Patty in the movie, and that seemed to be Winona's assessment of the film.

After the film was completed, Winona was her usual honest self. "I don't know how it turned out, but it wasn't a very good experience. It's the tale of a girl hidden at a boys' school. I didn't know how to play it well. You see I thought I knew and then I got to the set and realized I didn't know."

She sighed, "This was my attempt at trying to get back to those independent type of films like *Heathers*, but it really didn't work out."

But how could it possibly go wrong if someone like Al Pacino is

Looking for Richard

YEAR: *1996*

STARING:
Alec Baldwin, Kenneth Branagh, John Gielgud, James Earl Jones, Kevin Kline, Al Pacino, Aidan Quinn, Vanessa Redgrave, Winona Ryder, and Kevin Spacey

BILLING:
*Tenth
(in alphabetical order)*

WRITTEN BY:
*Fred Kimball, Al Pacino, and William Shakespeare
(based on the play*
Richard III*)*

DIRECTED BY:
Al Pacino

PRODUCED BY:
Twentieth-Century Fox

RATING: *PG-13*

RUNNING TIME:
96 minutes

WINONA'S CHARACTER'S
NAME: *Lady Anne*

directing? That's a different story and a different sort of independent film. Although she wasn't destined to play Pacino's daughter in *Godfather III*, she did appear with him in a pivotal scene in his self-directed movie, *Looking for Richard*.

At fifty-six, the Oscar-winning Pacino wanted to produce an independent documentary that would help people understand Shakespeare and appreciate the playwright's *Richard III*. He went about his task by gathering up a bunch of movie stars, Shakespeare experts, and people on the street to playfully investigate the life and language of the play.

In *Looking for Richard*, Pacino said, "I try to explode the vintage Shakespeare. If the audience feels that it got a taste of Shakespeare, I'll have succeeded." The actor/director later said about the film, "To me it's an experiment. I wanted to see if I can get an audience accustomed to hearing that sound and eventually delivering some of these Shakespearean words in a way that is understood."

Pacino asked Winona to play Lady Anne in his play within a movie. She joined not only Pacino, but an illustrious cast that included Alec Baldwin, Kenneth Branagh, John Gielgud, James Earl Jones, Kevin Kline, Aidan Quinn, Vanessa Redgrave, and Kevin Spacey. The only problem was that she didn't know Pacino was making a movie! "I'm ready to strangle him," she said, "because he called me up—this was like four years ago— and said, 'Oh, come do this thing. It'll be fun. We'll just do a scene.' So,

now it's a movie and I'm mortified. It's actually a great movie, but I'm still mortified that I'm in it."

One of the reasons she may be so upset is that it isn't even her own voice that is heard on the soundtrack. Though she was reportedly up to the demands of Shakespeare's language, there was a problem with the sound recording and her vocal performance was lost. Rather than lose her extraordinary physical and facial performance as well, Pacino went ahead and dubbed Winona's voice with that of Richard Burton's actress daughter, Kate Burton.

No wonder Winona is mortified.

Winona looks at Al Pacino with a combination of apprehension and adoration in a movie she is both "mortified" to be in and proud of, all at the same time, *Looking for Richard.* PHOTO COURTESY OF TWENTIETH CENTURY FOX, © 1996.

CHAPTER 16

A Clone Again, Naturally

"We're finally getting her out of corsets."

—A WINONA
SPOKESPERSON ABOUT
HER ROLE IN *ALIEN 4*

For her next two projects, Winona decided to go against any other type she'd ever done before.

First, she played a young woman with a passion gone wild in *The Crucible* (1996), then she dove into the action genre (like her friends Keanu Reeves, Christian Slater, and Daniel Day-Lewis), by costarring with Sigourney Weaver (who plays a clone of herself; her character in *Alien 3* died) in *Alien 4* (1997). In both, Winona plays misfits.

The Crucible was directed by Nicholas Hytner, the man who stunned the Academy Awards by receiving some top nominations for his spectacular period film *The Madness of King George* (1994). The project had been bandied about for years: Back in 1991, Canadian director Norman Jewison wanted to adopt the play and at one point it was a project that Kenneth Branagh considered.

The story is an adaptation of Arthur Miller's classic 1953 play about the Salem witch trials of the seventeenth

Winona plays Abigail, the "bad girl" in Arthur Miller's *The Crucible*. PHOTO BY BARRY WETCHER, TWENTIETH CENTURY FOX, © 1996.

century. Winona, as Abigail Williams, accuses her enemies of witchcraft in the film that was released in December 1996.

Director Hytner had only one film behind him, although it was an exceptional one, and he said he was nervous since the screenwriter was the same Arthur Miller. "It's downright terrifying," he said. "It was like going to Shakespeare and asking for amendments to King Lear."

During filming of *The Crucible* at the remote Hog Island, near Essex, Massachusetts, the quiet local residents weren't thrilled when Hollywood blustered into town—even though local tours were given of the outside of Daniel Day-Lewis's rented house for twenty bucks! And the local clam crop just about stopped when the cast and crew arrived.

One resident whined, "I've got kids to feed. We like Hollywood, we like renting movies, but we like our clammers better." But the movie folk actually contributed to the local clam economy, at least in a small way,

The Crucible

YEAR: *1996*

STARRING:
*Daniel Day-Lewis,
Winona Ryder,
Joan Allen, and
Paul Scofield*

BILLING:
Second

WRITTEN BY:
*Arthur Miller,
based on his play*

DIRECTED BY:
Nicholas Hytner

PRODUCED BY:
Twentieth Century-Fox

RATING: *PG-13*

RUNNING TIME:
96 minutes

WINONA'S
CHARACTER'S NAME:
Abigail Williams

because in one scene, one of the accused women is seen digging for clams. So the crew waded across the channel, bought some clams, and used them in the movie as props.

Winona was surrounded by some class actors during the filming. The woman nominated for a Best Supporting Actress Oscar for her role as Pat Nixon in *Nixon* (1996), Joan Allen, stars in the film as Elizabeth Proctor, and other cast members included Frances Conroy as Ann Putnam, Jeffrey Jones as Thomas Putnam, Paul Scofield as Judge John Danforth, and Rob Campbell as Reverend Hale.

We caught up to Winona just before *The Crucible* opened to rave reviews. You can read the interview on page 180.

Folks around Hollywood are still scratching their heads about *Alien Resurrection*, and why Winona would sign on to such a project. People are even surprised Sigourney Weaver agreed to come back, since she was quoted after *Alien 3* as saying, "This is it, I die in this one and Ripley is not coming back. There's no way."

Actually, there is a way to die and come back—if you're cloned. And, if you have a hot-looking sidekick android who looks like Winona Ryder (and it helps when you get an $11 million paycheck.). It should be one heck of a dynamic duo doing battle against the face-hugging, chest-bursting, acid-bleeding beasts. They could be a female fighting team sensation.

French director Jean-Pierre Jeunet was chosen to direct his first English-language film with this fourth *Alien* episode and Tom Sherak, senior executive vice president at Fox, said that although *Alien 3* wasn't a major hit and picked up only $56 million, the audience might still be around, especially after the alien frenzy of the film *Independence Day* (1996). The second *Alien* sequel opened huge at twenty-three million dollars compared with the first *Alien*'s ten million dollars.

The new *Alien* will have to far surpass its predecessor to recoup its $70 million budget. Many people called Winona "the last one you'd expect to see on the final frontier," but she seems happy to team up and take on the season's highly anticipated *Batman* feature as this alien monster becomes Earthbound. Winona landed a $3–$5 million paycheck for her role.

Bruce Davison as Reverend Parris becomes embroiled in Winona's plans for revenge. PHOTO BY BARRY WETCHER, TWENTIETH CENTURY FOX, © 1996.

Winona received some of the best reviews of her career for her performance in *The Crucible*.
PHOTO BY BARRY WETCHER, TWENTIETH CENTURY FOX, © 1996.

Winona's Colleagues Pick Her Best Performances

DAVID SCHWIMMER, ACTOR: *Welcome Home, Roxy Carmichael.* "I know she was a lot younger in that, but I really liked that movie. I thought she was great."

GWYNETH PALTROW, ACTRESS: *Reality Bites.* "I thought she was fantastic, really funny, natural, and very cool in that movie."

TERI HATCHER, ACTRESS: *Little Women.* "I thought she was pretty great. The older she gets, the more and more interesting she's going to be. She's a spectacular actress."

QUENTIN TARANTINO, WRITER/DIRECTOR/ACTOR: *Great Balls of Fire!* "She breaks my heart in that movie."

JOEL COEN, DIRECTOR/WRITER: *The Age of Innocence.* "She was great. She's a terrific actress; I really like her. The only problem I had with her in *Little Women* was one of her sisters says that her hair is her only asset, which I thought was a little weird in reference to Winona Ryder. She has more going for her in the looks department than her hair."

ETHAN COEN, WRITER/PRODUCER: *Beetlejuice.* "She was really funny as a junior Morticia."

Winona and Charlayne Woodard act out a secret ceremony in an early scene from *The Crucible*. PHOTO BY BARRY WETCHER, TWENTIETH CENTURY FOX, © 1996.

Winona is the leader of the pack. PHOTO BY BARRY WETCHER, TWENTIETH CENTURY FOX, © 1996.

Winona on Being Interviewed

"I wouldn't flirt with the people who interview me,
but sometimes they write about me in kind of a sexual way,
and that's really weird to me because I'm not like that
when I'm interviewing. I save that for my private life.
I don't try to kind of show myself that way. Maybe because
I'm young, they want to make me out to be this Lolita,
this woman-child. I don't know. I think it's kind of weird.
That's why I'm much more careful now with the writers
who are going to do a feature story on me. I really like
kind of have them checked out, you know?"

Back with Daniel Day-Lewis, with whom she last worked in *The Age of Innocence*, Winona plays a woman scorned, giving a terrifyingly vivid performance in *The Crucible*. PHOTO BY BARRY WETCHER, TWENTIETH CENTURY FOX, © 1996.

The Bewitching Winona Ryder

Generation X has a reputation for being essentially illiterate, yet its leading actress, Winona Ryder, has, ironically, largely built her career and made her reputation on films based on classic literature and theater, from *Little Women* to *Bram Stoker's Dracula*, from *The Age of Innocence* to her latest film, *The Crucible*. Of all of these projects, it is Arthur Miller's *The Crucible* that has both stretched her abilities as an actress the most and has brought her her greatest sense of achievement.

Extraordinarily delicate in person, Winona Ryder glided into a New York hotel room like a leaf on a gentle breeze. Her large eyes framed on a smooth face, save for a faded scar above her left eyebrow, she looked eagerly at her questioners, anxious to talk about her work in a film that has clearly meant a great deal to her. In the film she plays Abigail, the tempestuous young woman who begins the Salem witch-hunts in order, at first, to save herself from punishment, and then later to accuse John Proctor's wife of witchcraft in order to have Proctor (Daniel Day-Lewis) for herself.

"The great challenge of [playing Abigail] was that I never, in my career, played a person who you didn't either root for somewhat or feel sorry for," she began. More than that, she said, she had to convincingly convey a character who was "full of confusion and contradictions. I couldn't just play her as a bitch, which is what a lot of people ask. 'What was it like, playing the bitch?' I didn't see her as that. I actually did understand where she was coming from in the beginning of the film. If you look at the situation, she's a young girl who's having this affair with an older married man. Then, suddenly he says, 'We never touched! 'Don't talk to me! Go away!'

"It's not a time [seventeeth-century Salem] where you can go, 'Well, I accept that.' It's also not a time when you can express yourself in any way at all when you're a girl that age. So she's devastated and crushed and hurt. She starts off so angry, and her reaction is almost understandable. It's what it becomes that's so out of control. Then, all of a sudden, she's given a voice. This girl has never mattered, but now this girl is a star and everyone is hanging on her every word. With that power, she, of course, starts to enjoy it. I don't think she's even realizing what's happening. But then I think she starts to believe her own lies. I think she became loony. What was so difficult about the role for me was I had to go from being very calculating, knowing exactly what I'm doing, like sticking a needle in my belly, to really believing that I'm a saint, that I'm here to cleanse the village. It was crazy going back and forth like that. In some scenes I was physically acting like a sinner but I was saying that I'm a saint."

There was yet another challenge for the young actress. She was totally intimidated by Arthur Miller, who both wrote the classic play and adapted it for the screen. "It's no fault of his," she laughed, admitting how cowed she was in his presence. "He's one of the warmest, kindest, put-you-at-ease, encouraging people. But it doesn't matter. It's Arthur Miller. I think he's the greatest playwright of this century. I've read all of his plays. I was a huge fan. I wanted to do *The Crucible* since I was twelve years old. I wanted to play Abigail. It was really something I wanted to do for over ten years."

Her connection with Miller is intensely personal. "He was a hero of my father's. My godfather, Timothy Leary, in the sixties experienced a lot of witch-hunting, and Arthur Miller, was the head of PEN [an influential writer's organization] at that time, and he actually wrote a letter in behalf of my godfather. That letter is framed in my dad's office."

When she read her role for the first time, she actually read it with Miller reading the Judge Danforth role. "I think I just stuttered my way through the first day's read through," she said. Later, during filming, she knew that Miller was often watching. "I just wanted to know what Arthur thought. And when you do finally get the thumbs up from him, you can die now, you know?"

Despite the fact that this is a period piece, Ryder acknowledged that this was her most sexual role to date. "It was great," she laughed, "because it was an opportunity to do it without taking my clothes off and getting sprayed with glycerin and roll around with somebody. To me, it was much more sexual than that. It was a different kind of sexuality. It was very aggressive, which was new." At that last comment she laughed, even as she blushed.

It was easier for her to do the love scenes in this movie, she said, because she was acting against Daniel Day-Lewis, with whom she also performed in *The Age of Innocence*. "It was great going into it, knowing how he works. When you're opposite him, he really has you by the throat. He doesn't let you falter or slip away. It's impossible not to be in the moment with him; he insists on it. He forces you to rise to his level, which is almost impossible to rise to." And in case you're wondering, she also added, "He's just a great person, a really nice guy."

Preparing for this role was an ordeal for Ryder. "I did more research and rehearsals than I've ever done," she said. "There was a lot of preparation, but the emotional preparation, which I couldn't even begin to talk about because I don't understand it myself, was pretty excruciating. It's a painful part to play. Usually when I work on a movie I'm able to do a scene and then relax for a little while, and then go back and do another angle of it. With the exception of *The Age of Innocence*, this was the first time I couldn't relax, ever. Every scene, every angle, and every shot, I'm either screaming or crying or flailing around in the water or something. It was very exhausting, and not something you could let go of at the end of the day. We were all walking around like zombies throughout much of the shoot." In fact, she said, "I played the last act of the movie like a junkie withdrawing."

This Generation X movie star will likely continue to appear in period pieces and adaptations of classic literature, though it won't be by design. "If *Little Women* or *The Crucible* or any of those others had taken place in this era and had been as well written, I would have been thrilled [to do them]," she said. "It's not that I love to be in a corset; I don't, I hate it."

On the other hand, she said, "I think there's something about a time when people had to communicate face-to-face, one-on-one, that really appeals to me. [In the classics] there's usually better dialogue, and more dialogue; it's like, give me more lines. An actor's dream is lines, lines, lines. And I've always loved the classics. I'd love to do something contemporary. I mean I beg for it. But the contemporary scripts I get sent a lot of the time are just really bad. They just don't churn out very good scripts, so when you have something like *The Crucible* or *The Age of Innocence,* or something based on a great book, it's just a lot richer."

She joked that her next film, *Alien Resurrection,* is also a period piece, although the period is in the future. She's terribly excited about doing it, she said, "because I'm a huge sci-fi fan."

She was less than ten years old when she saw the original *Alien* (1979) with Sigourney Weaver. "It was the first time I ever saw a female action hero. It's a brilliant movie. Everyone, I think, will agree. So, I've always loved that series [i.e. *Alien,* it's sequel, *Aliens* (1986), and *Alien 3* (1992)]." She pointed out that, as a rule, she doesn't like violent movies, "but when it's not human-to-human violence, I can take it." In *Alien Resurrection,* she said, "It's like human to monster/alien violence, so it's more acceptable to me." Though she said, "I'm actually not supposed to talk about it. They've literally made me sign something." She did allow, however, that "I'm not playing the creature."

CHAPTER 17

Quirky Winona

"Quirky.
If anyone
ever calls me
quirky again,
I think they
should be shot."

—WINONA TO *ROLLING STONE* MAGAZINE, ABOUT A WORD THAT SHOULDN'T BE USED TO DESCRIBE HER.

She's odd, she's goofy, she's a nerd, she's a sorta geek, but she's beautiful. But, never never *ever* call her quirky. She is quirky, but don't tell her that to her face. Some of the reasons she is and forever will be considered quirky are obvious.

❦ When writer Ian Hamilton wrote an unauthorized prying biography of her literary hero, the reclusive *Catcher in the Rye* author J. D. Salinger, Winona wrote a smarmy, short, bogus biography of Hamilton and sent it to him, "just to show you," she wrote, "what it feels like." She did get a Christmas card signed by Salinger, but she wondered if she should return it to him, and she did.

❦ She goes to thrift stores to buy charm bracelets, spider pins, funky hats, vests, *Batman* comic books, antique pocket watches, vintage men's suits, and retro sunglasses.

Winona is mesmerizing when she looks exotic. PHOTO COURTESY OF MOVIE STAR NEWS.

❣ Although she's tiring of corsets, she loves to dress up. "The funnest thing to do is to dress up," Ryder said. "But nothing ever fits me, because I'm so small."

❣ She doesn't like flying on planes at all. On her nineteenth birthday she was going to fly somewhere, but drove instead. "That was the day Randy Rhodes [Ozzy Osbourne's guitarist] died in a plane crash. I've tried to avoid flying ever since then." She also said she once freaked out on a plane and a stewardess had to hold her throughout most of a whole flight.

❣ Her superstitions often get the best of her. She dreamt that director Richard Attenborough had died in a plane that crashed against a snowy mountain. She called Attenborough's office to tell him not to fly that day. Although he had already switched a scheduled flight, the plane he had been booked on did crash—against a snowy mountain.

❣ She still has this old hobby of discovering abandoned houses. "We just started doing it for fun. Instead of going to a party, we'd find an abandoned house, roam around, and tell ghost stories. It's really romantic if you get to do it with guys, but I never get to do it with guys."

She will always remain a good storyteller, with a slight embellishment here and there, according to her family. She also dove into the new computer superhighway, thanks to her godfather Tim Leary, who was a pioneer with the interactive computer system and died online after he was diagnosed with terminal cancer.

On the internet, Winona had her own Web site, but it got too crazy because of the thousands of hits she was getting from across the globe. She felt a responsibility to answer each person, but it took too much of her time and she signed off. Now there are dozens of Web sites specifically geared to her, where people rate their favorite Winona films and download their favorite Winona photos. (Read on for more details.)

The least favorite of her films among the fans are her first film *Lucas*, *Boys*, and *1969*. The all-around favorite is overwhelmingly *Heathers*, with *Mermaids* and *Reality Bites* a distant second and third.

On one movie poll on the internet, of 573 people, the first Winona Ryder movie most fans saw was *Beetlejuice*, followed by *Bram Stoker's Dracula*, then *Heathers*. For a vote on the screen couple people most wanted to see together, Winona and Keanu Reeves came in second only to Sharon Stone and Brad Pitt. Several video clips from Winona's movies can also be downloaded to one's home computer.

On the Web site dedicated to Winona based in Finland, one angry fan wrote: "In my country (Finland) *How to Make an American Quilt* is not so popular. They are showing it in the small movie theater. I think it's one of the best Winona movies. So I'm little bit angry, cos [sic] they think that no one cares about that movie!"

Her fans are passionate about her, even online.

Results From the Winona Ryder Web Site Survey

More than 1,000 responded to this survey.

DEMOGRAPHICS
19.4 percent Female
80.6 percent Male

AGE
0.3 percent below 13
7.7 percent 13–17
51.1 percent 18–25
33.0 percent 26–40
7.9 percent over 40

WINONA'S MOST POPULAR FILMS
(by vote on a scale of 1–10)
8.0 *Heathers*
7.9 *Little Women*
7.5 *How to Make an American Quilt*
7.4 *Edward Scissorhands*
7.3 *The Age of Innocence*
7.3 *Bram Stoker's Dracula*
7.2 *Beetlejuice*
7.2 *Reality Bites*
7.0 *Mermaids*
6.9 *Night on Earth*
6.8 *The House of the Spirits*
6.3 *1969*
6.3 *Great Balls of Fire!*
6.1 *Lucas*

6.1 *Welcome Home, Roxy Carmichael*
5.7 *Square Dance*

MOST SEEN FILMS (out of 975 voters)
741 *Beetlejuice*
730 *Edward Scissorhands*
699 *Bram Stoker's Dracula*
602 *Reality Bites*
590 *Mermaids*
583 *Heathers*
495 *Little Women*
483 *Great Balls of Fire!*
467 *The Age of Innocence*
449 *Welcome Home, Roxy Carmichael*
339 *Lucas*
324 *The House of the Spirits*
260 *Night on Earth*
244 *1969*
241 *How to Make an American Quilt*
137 *Square Dance*

FIRST MOVIE SEEN STARRING WINONA RYDER
37.4 *Beetlejuice*
17.1 *Lucas*
12.7 *Heathers*
5.4 *Edward Scissorhands*
3.3 *Mermaids*
3.2 *Great Balls of Fire!*
3.1 *Bram Stoker's Dracula*
2.2 *Reality Bites*
1.8 *Welcome Home, Roxy Carmichael*
1.1 *The Age of Innocence*
1.1 *Little Women*
1.1 *Night on Earth*
0.7 *The House of the Spirits*
0.8 *Square Dance*
0.6 *1969*
0.3 *How to Make an American Quilt*
7.7 had not seen a movie with Winona Ryder in it(?!)

Internet Sites

There are dozens of Winona Ryder sites on the Internet. Here are some of the most popular ones.

ERIC HARSHBARGER'S WINONA PAGE (this one is known and widely touted as the most accurate, most interesting, and "the ultimate")

http://www.auburn.edu/~harshec/WWW/Winona.html

WINONA RYDER PAGE, a dreamy photo archive with text in English and Hungarian (native language of the site's founder)

http://www.sch.bme.hu/~joker/winona.html

Other hot sites

Albert Yau's Winona Ryder pictures
alt.binaries.pictures.celebrities
alt.cult-movies: Movies with a cult following
alt.fan.actors: Discussion of actors and actresses
alt.fan.winona-ryder: Gen-X Gorgeous Elfin Brainy Goddess Actress
alt.society.generation-x: Lifestyles of those born 1960–early–1970s
Another page (Japan)
Art Whitehead's Winona Ryder Gallery page
B.D. Decker's Winona page
Big Al's Winona page
Brett Kokegei's Winona Archive
Brian D. Decker's page (Herndon, Virginia)
Buena Vista/Touchstone Pictures Web Site for *Boys*
Chris Franklin's page (College Station, Texas)
Christian Bale Homepage (co-star with Winona Ryder in *Little Women*)
clari.apbl.movies: News on movies and filmmaking
clari.living.movies: News of film and movies
David Sok's page
Heathers fans, http://www.best.com/~sirlou/heathers.shtml
Heathers site by Louis Kahn
How to Make an American Quilt site by MCA/Universal
http://ccwf.cc.utexas.edu/~duongrn/winona.html
http://chem.leeds.ac.uk/ICAMS/people/jon/winona.html

http://www.access.digex.net/~bdecker/afwr.html
http://www.auburn.edu/~harshec/WWW/Winona.html
http://www.chem.surrey.ac.uk:80/~ch02jb/winona.html
http://www.cica.indiana.edu/~scotto/movies/win/Winona.html
http://www.clark.net/pub/phil/WinonaRyder.html
http://www.isd.uni-stuttgart.de/~breitfeld/winona.html
http://www.phoenix.net/~sierra/winona.html
http://www.umich.edu/~vrmjay/articles.html
Kurniawan's page (Indonesia)
Luminous Winona
Magnus Lundquist's Winona Ryder Picture Gallery
Michael's Beauty Appreciation Pages
Nicolas Pelletier page (Quebec, Canada)
Patrick's Winona Ryder Page
Phil Anglin (phil@clark.net)
Polly Klaas Foundation: http://www.northcoast.com/klaas/klaas.html
Reality Bites site by Joanna Vaught
rec.arts.movies.reviews: Reviews of movies
Richard Miller's page (Netherlands)
Scott Farmer's page
Sierra's Winona Ryder page
Star Bios Facts
Ted Yee's page (Vancouver, Canada)
Thorsten Breitfeld's page (Stuttgart, Germany)
Vijay Ramanujan's Winona Articles
Who else but Winona?
Winona Ryder ("Ein Amerikanischer Quilt")
Winona Ryder Central Link Page
Winona Ryder Gallery
Winona Ryder Heaven
Zeb's WWW page for Winona Ryder

The Internet is constantly changing and some of the sites may no longer exist. However, some additional sites may have been added. Your best bet is to use a trusty entertainment search engine (like Alta Vista, Webcrawler, or Yahoo!) to find your favorite Winona Ryder site. Many clips from Winona's most popular movies can also be downloaded from the Internet.

It was on the set of *Edward Scissorhands* that Winona, looking unnaturally blond, began her tempestuous romance with Johnny Depp. PHOTO BY ZADE ROSENTHAL, TWENTIETH CENTURY FOX, © 1990.

Just like in *Square Dance*, Winona plays a character in *Roxy Carmichael* who figures to get out of town. PHOTO COURTESY OF PHOTOFEST.

Winona was just getting warmed up for her look in period costumes in *Dracula*. The best was yet to come. PHOTO COURTESY OF PHOTOFEST.

CHAPTER 18

The Star's the Limit

"It's okay to be who I am. It's okay to be a fucking movie star. It's okay to live in a nice house."

—WINONA IN A RECENT INTERVIEW IN *PREMIERE* MAGAZINE

Very few times does anyone's personal and professional lives completely coincide and coexist. Usually, when one is good, the other is miserable, and vice-versa. Right now, Winona is in a pretty good space both professionally and personally, and she knows that's a rare occurrence, both for her and for most people.

Right now, personally, she said she's happy with her boyfriend, Dave Pirner. He treats her well, he's relaxed, and they have no plans for anything more than living together. The reality is that he is a hard-working musician dedicated to his craft—and he appears to be dedicated to Winona.

Pirner assesses their possible future marriage with, "Well, yeah I think about it. Everybody who's got a girlfriend should think about it. It surprises me that more people don't take a look in the mirror a little more often and assess their own relationships. I mean don't people in

A devastating young beauty, Winona would have to wait just a bit longer to play her own age.
PHOTO COURTESY OF MOVIE STAR NEWS.

the paparazzi have girlfriends and stuff? Where's the common courtesy? Pretty simple stuff."

Her reply: "God, I'm very happy that I'm not with an actor. I hate generalizations, and actually I know some of the most wonderful actors who are kind and not involved in things that are gross, or the 'scene,' or whatever. Yet it is nice that my boyfriend does this other thing I find totally fascinating and that there's no competition [between us] at all."

She talked about having children, telling one reporter, "I can't wait to have kids. I want little boys. Want to hear the names I'm gonna name them? I like baseball names. Vida Blue Ryder. Cool Papa Ryder. Unless I marry some guy that has a better last name than me."

Maybe she's given it up only recently, but she's not smoking and she isn't chewing her nails anymore. She certainly hasn't experimented with drugs or destroyed any hotel rooms.

Winona has been stalked. It was scary for her (as it would be for anyone) and the security officials who guard her say it's not wise to discuss it because it only gives the criminals ammunition and adds to their obsessive behaviors. She is often guarded when out in public, although it isn't obvious.

She said she would love to direct her own film someday. "I've fantasized about it. I've learned so much about good directing from bad directing." She has directed a video, completed in August 1995, for a documentary of her boyfriend Pirner.

On a sad note, she gave the eulogy for her godfather, Timothy Leary, who died of cancer on May 31, 1996. She was devastated over the death of the Harvard psychologist who advocated the use of safe mind-altering drugs. The ceremony took place in a battered airport hangar in Santa Monica and lasted for about two hours.

Winona's message was simple: "He was the first person who made me believe I could do anything. What I learned from him wasn't about drugs, it was about getting by."

Ram Dass, a noted spiritual leader also spoke, then a video tribute to him set to Beatles music was shown. Winona did sob, and her eyes were wet when she led the people out the doors.

Professionally, she's commanding a higher salary than ever. The average grosses that her movies attract, as reported in *Entertainment Weekly* in April 1996, are $36 million domestic, $30 million foreign. It has been said that she "has outclassed her contemporaries by aiming high" and that she is getting between $3 and $5 million per picture. The magazine suggested that her asking price should be more, at around $5.4 million.

Her ex, Johnny Depp, scored lower, not selling as many tickets and is asking $5 million but should get just $3.5 million, *Entertainment Weekly* reported.

This year, Fox Studios brought out a bevy of stars to Las Vegas to promote upcoming projects. It was the first ShoWest convention at which Winona appeared since she won Star of Tomorrow Award with Johnny in 1990. She appeared on one stage with Sandra Bullock, Arnold Schwarzenegger, Warren Beatty, Morgan Freeman, Jeff Goldblum, Tom Hanks, Howie Long, Bill Pullman, Keanu Reeves, Meg Ryan, Will Smith, Liv Tyler, Sigourney Weaver, and Garth Brooks.

She's optioned her first screenplay, co-written with *Beetlejuice* screenwriter Michael McDowell, which she described as "a corny romance, almost a satire, about a girl who works in a bobby-pin factory whose dreams come true." No word yet when that project will be developed.

Despite what people may see on the Internet, Winona has not, nor will she ever, appear nude on film. There are several allegedly nude photos of her floating around the net, but computer goons, even with unsophisticated programs, can easily manipulate any image.

An overly-irritated director Kathryn Bigelow almost completely gave up the good-ol'-boy Hollywood system to go independent with her pet project about Joan of Arc in which she wanted Winona to star. It seems that the guys don't think a butch Winona in a crewcut will cut it at the box office, despite her super roles of late and accolades for her in short hair in *How to*

Make an American Quilt. Recently, Winona bowed out of the part and recommended her friend Claire Danes for the role. (We wonder: does Claire have greater appeal?) Sighed Bigelow, "I've resorted to trying to tell the studio execs that it [the film] has a lot of blood and violence."

On February 23, 1996 Winona left her longtime agency, Creative Artists Agency in favor of Carol Bodie, in charge of Three Arts Entertainment. She also got flooded with scripts.

What sequel would Winona most like to see made to one of her past movies? Not much could be done with *Lucas*, or *Bram Stoker's Dracula*, or *The Age of Innocence* but Michael Keaton recently expressed interest in a *Beetlejuice* sequel—and maybe a grown-up "little girl who dresses in black" could appear in it again. Her ultimate dream, however, which was reiterated in July 1996, was that she would make a sequel to *Heathers*.

There's also talk of a Twentieth Century Fox project on the horizon. The studio bought rights to the book *The Trials of Maria Barbella*, an Idanna Pucci period piece, and they want Winona to star in it. The story concerns a turn-of-the-century trial of two falsely accused women.

Another project Winona is strongly considering is a part in the film *Girl Interrupted*, directed by Jocelyn Moorhouse, with whom she got along so well while making *How to Make an American Quilt*. The script,

The Winona Ryder S. A. T.

(Scrapbook Aptitude Test)

Now that you've read and (we hope!) enjoyed *The Winona Ryder Scrapbook,* why not test your knowledge of Noni?

1. WINONA GOT HER NAME FROM:
    a. a town named Ryder
    b. a named suggested by her godfather
    c. a town named Winona
    d. a truck rental company.

2. THE TATTOO ON JOHNNY DEPP'S BODY REFERRING TO WINONA READS:
    a. Winona My Love
    b. Winona Forever
    c. Winona This Hurts
    d. None of the above

3. WITH WHICH ONE OF THE FOLLOWING ACTORS DID WINONA SHARE THE SCREEN IN TWO DIFFERENT FILMS?
    a. Charlie Sheen
    b. Gabriel Byrne
    c. Michael Keaton
    d. Daniel Day-Lewis

4. WINONA WAS NOMINATED FOR A BEST ACTRESS OSCAR FOR HER PERFORMANCE IN:
    a. *Little Women*
    b. *The Age of Innocence*
    c. *Edward Scissorhands*
    d. None of the above

5. WHO REPLACED WINONA WHEN SHE DROPPED OUT OF *THE GODFATHER PART III*?
    a. Sofia Coppola
    b. Bridget Fonda
    c. rewritten for Mario Donatone
    d. None of the above

6. WINONA PLAYS "THE OLDER WOMAN" IN WHICH ONE OF THE FOLLOWING MOVIES?
   a. *Welcome Home, Roxy Carmichael*
   b. *Square Dance*
   c. *Boys*
   d. *Mermaids*

7. *SQUARE DANCE* HAS BEEN SHOWN ON TELEVISION WITH THE FOLLOWING DIFFERENT TITLE:
   a. *Home is Where the Heart Is*
   b. *Dosey Doe Your Partner*
   c. *Barn Dance*
   d. *Hitching a Ride*

8. WHAT WAS THE NAME OF WINONA'S CHARACTER IN *GREAT BALLS OF FIRE!*?
   a. Bobbie Sue
   b. Rita
   c. Jo
   d. Myra

9. WINONA HAS NOT DATED:
   a. Robert Sean Leonard
   b. Christian Slater
   c. Gary Oldman
   d. David Pirner

10. WHAT MOVIE DID HER AGENT WARN WINONA AGAINST STARRING IN, TELLING HER IT WOULD DESTROY HER CAREER?
    a. *Boys*
    b. *Heathers*
    c. *Great Balls of Fire!*
    d. *Beetlejuice*

Answers

(Scrapbook Aptitude Test)

1. c   2. b   3. d
(*The Age of Innocence* and *The Crucible*)
4. a (she was also nominated for *The Age of Innocence* but that was for Best Supporting Actress; she did not win either time.)
5. a   6. c   7. a
8. d   9. c   10. b

191

What Winona Has to Say About Her Costars and Directors

Cher	"Fun"
Susan Sarandon	"Tough, hard-working and spirited"
Geena Davis	"Goofy"
Meryl Streep	"The most beautiful woman in the world"
Michelle Pfeiffer	"Exquisite"
Rob Lowe	"Nice"
Daniel Day-Lewis	"Be still my beating heart"
Johnny Depp	"Um, weird"
Jeremy Irons	"Surprisingly funny"
Christian Slater	"Really comfortable with himself"
Anthony Hopkins	"The best we have today, brilliant"
Francis Ford Coppola	"Jovial, yet intense"
Martin Scorsese	"Greatest director on the planet"
Tim Burton	"Greatest director off the planet"

cowritten by Lisa Loomer and Susan Shilliday, is based on a true story about a problem teenager of the 1950s who is banished by her parents to a mental institution. She is also interested in the film *Roustabout*, but it's pending script changes.

The director who would most love to work with her again is Tim Burton, who directed her in both *Beetlejuice* and *Edward Scissorhands*. He said her future is bright. "In her teens, she offered something nobody else could and she'll do that in her adult roles. I'm not worried about Winona. She'll do just fine."

She is sad, sometimes nostalgic, that she has to keep inside the privacy of her own home a lot, but she tries to keep her life as normal as possible, despite her burgeoning fame.

"The only time I ever feel like I'm in the business is when I go somewhere public and there are photographers saying my name; I get a really weird chill," Winona said. "I wish I could sit and think about it, but every time I do I get so nervous that I end up changing the subject. Sometimes I really sort of resent what I've gotten myself into."

As a result of her fame, she doesn't go out that often. She's a rare sight at a Hollywood premiere, but she'll often go with friends to a local movie house and stand in line, practically incognito.

Her love for anything Italian, too, caused her to make an appearance at a special Italian ceremony. "What is my favorite thing about Italy?" Anjelica Huston smiled hungrily as she sat down with Winona. "Pasta!" Huston was honored along with Richard Dreyfuss and director Francis Ford Coppola by the Republic of Italy at the Rudoph Valentino Awards held recently at the Century Plaza Hotel, and *US* magazine was invited to sit with them.

"It's nice to know that I and some guy who's been dubbing me in Italy have been honored tonight," joked Dreyfuss to Winona. Then, as Coppola passed by, Dreyfuss broke out into *The Godfather* theme and Winona gave the director a big kiss and hug. "I always said I'd never go along with these lifetime achievement awards, but this is my culture," the director said about receiving the Italian version of the Oscar. Sofia Coppola said to Winona that she was recently wowed after seeing her father's film *Apoca-lypse Now* in a theater for the first time. Seated at the large table with Winona were Marsha Mason, Martin Sheen, Jon Voight, and the whole cast of the soap opera *The Bold and the Beautiful*, which is Italy's top rated show. They dined on breaded veal, Italian wine, goat cheese, and lots of pasta.

Winona was truly quiet that night. "It's not my award tonight, I'd really not like to talk," she said to media. Her ex, Johnny Depp, was supposed to be there, but didn't show. She simply said, "I am here for Francis."

Winona's legacy on the entertainment industry is only now being realized. Johnny Depp predicted, "Winona may be the Lillian Gish of the next century. I see her in 2040 still doing movies. She's got that much time and energy left . . . and it's hard to calm her down when she likes something."

She remains a movie star in the truest sense of the word: classy, beautiful, warm, dedicated, and luminous, and she brings with her attributes that few other celebrities have: intelligence, friendliness, and approachability.

That's all only in her first quarter century of life.

Her performance in *The Age of Innocence* brought her a Golden Globe Award for Best Supporting Actress. PHOTO BY MICHAEL FERGUSON, GLOBE PHOTOS, INC., © 1994.

Winona didn't win the Best Supporting Actress award at the 66th Annual Oscars, but she sure turned a lot of heads, establishing herself as an Oscar fashion trendsetter.

PHOTO BY MICHAEL FERGUSON, GLOBE PHOTOS, INC., © 1994.

S cott and Barbara Siegel are the authors of forty-six books, including *The Jim Carrey Scrapbook* (Citadel Press, 1995), *American Film Comedy* (Macmillan, 1994), and *The Encyclopedia of Hollywood* (Facts on File in hardcover, 1990; Avon Books in trade paperback, 1991). They have also written a considerable number of celebrity biographies, including those of Jack Nicholson, Bruce Willis, and Cybill Shepherd. The Siegels are film critics, whose reviews can be heard on the radio across the U.S. In addition, Scott and Barbara write a weekly theater and cabaret column for *Drama-Logue*.

Scott and Barbara organized, edited, and helped design the contents of this book, and penned a number of sidebar items, picked the photos, and wrote the captions as well. They interviewed a great many actors and directors about Winona, as well as interviewing Winona herself.

*T*his book could not have been written without the efforts of Michael Szymanski, who wrote the centerpiece of this volume, Winona's biography. He also contributed a great many of the sidebar items that grace the text. Szymanski is a highly respected freelance entertainment journalist who writes for the *Los Angeles Times,* the *New York Times Syndicate, Entertainment Weekly, US Magazine,* and a great many other publications. He provided the lead research for the Barbara Streisand biography written by James Spada.

Marty Martinez contributed research on Winona's rock and roll connections. The list of songs inspired by Winona Ryder is his work. Marty is a well-known New York radio personality where he has hosted Mr. Marty's All-Night Party on WNEW-FM. Marty is also the writer, producer, and host of the syndicated radio show "The Relix Bayrock Shop," which has been broadcast across the country since 1985. As an author, Marty has written approximately ninety articles, interviews, profiles, and reviews for the likes of *Relix, Traffic* and *Spin* magazines.

Raj Bahadur is responsible for the Q & A with Winona that appears in Chapter 11. That interview, as well as other research efforts, were of enormous help to this book. Raj is one of America's foremost entertainment correspondents, and his interviews regularly air on the Westwood One Radio Network. He is also a much respected film critic whose reviews can be found in *Screenscene* magazine.

ARTICLES ABOUT WINONA RYDER
USED IN THE WRITING OF THIS BOOK

MAGAZINES

American Film, January/February 1989.

Architectural Digest, May 1994; Pilar Viladas.

Blitz (UK), July 1991; Jonathan Bernstein.

British Vogue, February 1994; Phoebe Hoban.

Cahiers du Cinema (French), July/August 1991; Vincent Ostria.

Cinema (German), May 1995; Bert Brüllmann.

Cosmopolitan, August 1989; Susan Korones.

Current Biography, June 1994.

Drama-Logue, November 1996.

Elle, November 1990; Christa Worthington.

Empire (UK), June/July 1989.

Empire (UK), December 1989; Henri Behar.

Empire (UK), March 1993; Chris Heath et. al.

Empire (UK), February 1994; Chris Heath.

Empire (UK), July 1994; Jonathan Bernstein.

Empire, March 1995; Jeff Dawson.

Entertainment Weekly, February 10, 1994; Dana Kennedy.

Entertainment Weekly, December 23, 1994.

Entertainment Weekly, March 1995, (Special Academy Awards Issue).

Entertainment Weekly, October 3, 1995.

Esquire, April 1990; Paul Attanasio.

Esquire, November 1992; Michael Hirschorn.

The Face, November 1989; Steven Daly.

The Face (UK), July 1991.

The Face (UK), July 1994.

Film Monthly, May 1991; Edward Murphy.

Harper's Bazaar, September 1990; Kristine McKenna.

Harper's Bazaar, January 1991; Valerie Monroe.

Harper's Bazaar, December 1994; Polly Frost.

Interview, May 1989.

Interview, November 1989; Timothy Leary.

Interview, December 1990; Jeff Giles.

Ladies' Home Journal, December 1994; Meredith Berkman.

Life, June 1989.

Life, December 1994; Jenny Allen.

Marquee, June 1989; Nancy Mills.

Movieline, September 1995; Courtney Lee.

Newsweek, July 10, 1989; David Ansen.

New Woman, April 1994; Lisa Liebman.

People, October 6, 1995.

Premiere, June 1989; Phoebe Hoban.

Premiere, November 1990; Christopher Connelly.

Premiere, December 1992; Rachel Abramowitz.

Premiere, October 1993; Daphne Merkin.

Premiere, January 1995; Larissa MacFarquhar.

Premiere (France), June 1991; Aurelien Ferenczi.

Premiere (France), March 1995; Jean Paul Chaillet.

Premiere (UK), July 1994; Jeff Giles.

Prevue, February 1993.

Quake, Fall 1993.

Rolling Stone, May 8 1989; David Handelman.

Rolling Stone, December 3, 1990.

Rolling Stone, May 6, 1991; David Wild.

Rolling Stone, March 10, 1994; Jeff Giles.

Sassy, October 1988.

Select, July 1991; Lucy O'Brien.

Seventeen, October 1988; Edwin Miller.

Seventeen, December 1990; Claire Connors.

Sky International (UK), January 1993; Edwin J Bernard

Sky International (UK), January 1994; Edwin J. Bernard.

Sky Magazine (UK), November 1989; Phoebe Hoban.

Sky Magazine (UK), April 1991; Michael Kaplan.

Spy, December 1989.

Stern (Germany), April 25, 1991; Jochen Siemens.

Studio (France), April 1994.

'Teen, August 1989.

Time, May 1989; Chua-Eoan.

Time, December 1994.

Time, January 1995; Richard Corliss.

Time, April 1995.

Time, October 1995.

Time, December 1995.

Vanity Fair, April 1989.

Vogue, June 1989; Stephanie Mansfield.

Vogue, December 1990; Julia Reed.

Vogue, November 1992; Dario Scardapane.

Vogue, October 1993; David Handelman.

Who Weekly (Australia), April 10, 1995.

YM, March 1994; Dominique Das Cordobes.

NEWSPAPERS

Baltimore Sun, September 7, 1993.

Boston Globe, December 20, 1990.

Chicago Tribune, December, 1990; Michael Kaplan.

Dallas Morning News, November 7, 1992.

Guardian Weekend (UK), March 3, 1995; Joan Goodman.

Los Angeles Times, May 23, 1989; Patrick Goldstein.

Los Angeles Times, May 28, 1989; Kim Masters.

Los Angeles Times, December, 1990; Elaine Dutka.

New York Times, December, 1990; Aljean Harmetz.

San Francisco Chronicle, December 2, 1994.

San Francisco Chronicle, June 23, 1995.

San Francisco Chronicle, October 6, 1995.

San Francisco Examiner, October 8, 1993.

San Francisco Examiner, March 6, 1994; Joan Smith.

San Francisco Examiner, October 1, 1995.

USA Today, December 24, 1994; Karen Thomas.

*T*his book has had many friends along its path from conception to publication, chief among them Steven Schragis, our publisher. He wanted to do this book even before we did. His support, not to mention his vision, is very much appreciated. We'd also like to thank our patient editor, Mike Lewis, who, even though it was after our deadline, held up the production process so we could get a last-second interview with Winona and see her work in *The Crucible.*

We'd also like to give a nod of thanks to our fellow entertainment writers and broadcasters who gamely sat by while we asked any number of stars and directors about Winona Ryder when they had questions of their own. As for the interviewees, ranging from Susan Sarandon to Quentin Tarantino, thanks for your time and insights.

Finally, though, we thank Winona herself for providing us with so many outstanding performances in a career that, happily, has barely just begun.